DAILY VOCABULARY PRACTICE

Grade 2

Daily Vocabulary Practice provides a structured approach to building and reviewing your students' vocabulary skills.

Monthly Review
Apply skills learned each month

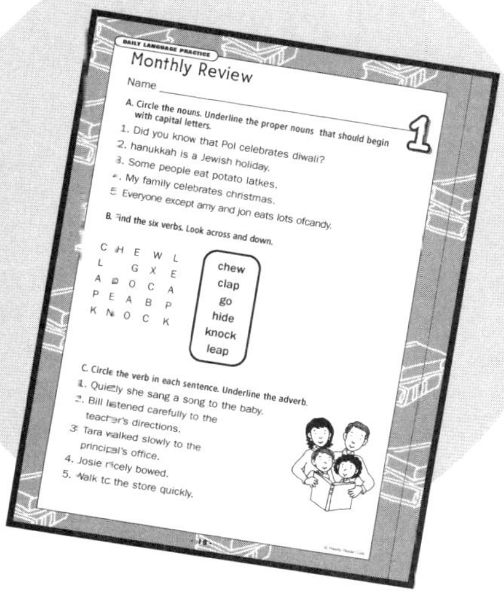

Weekly Skill
Practice one skill every day for a week

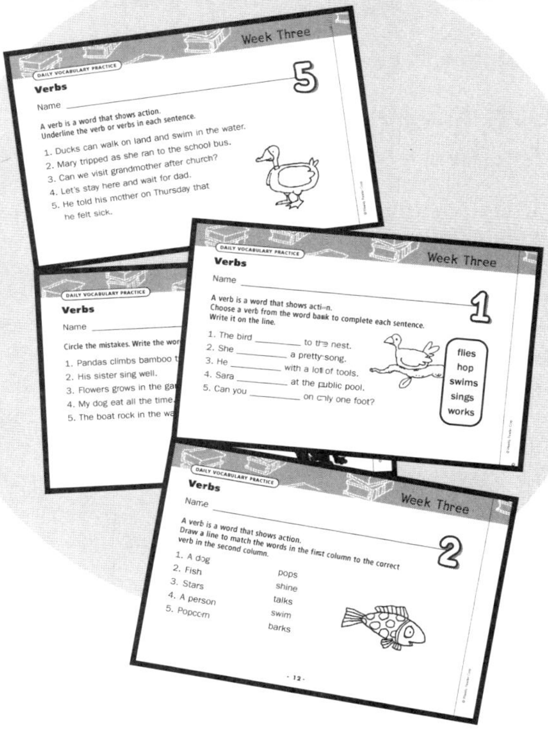

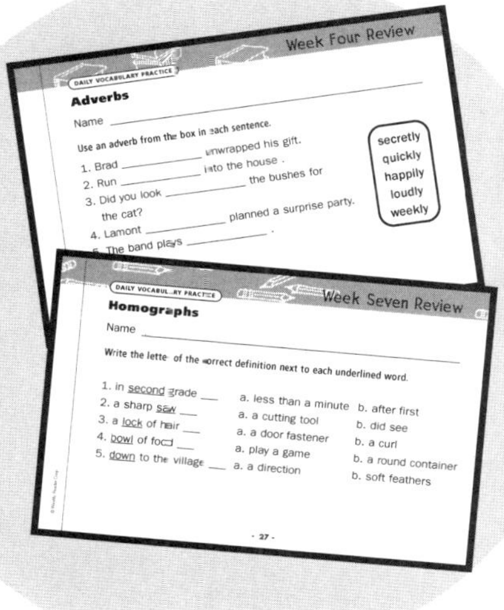

Weekly Review
Review weekly skill

ISBN: 9-780837-481265

1 2 3 4 5 / 10 09 08 07 06

Table of Contents

Using This Book

Good Vocabulary = Improved Reading Comprehension and Writing Skills

Did you know that vocabulary development is linked to improved reading comprehension? In this reproducible book you'll find daily vocabulary practice with essential second-grade words. It's a valuable classroom resource packed with quick and easy-to-use activities designed to strengthen vocabulary and build better readers. You can use these activities in a variety of classroom situations – as daily warm-ups, quick assessment tools, or helpful reviews.

The book's organization features 36 weekly practice sessions, followed by a monthly review of words covered in the previous weeks. This approach allows for in-depth and focused practice of essential vocabulary words in a concentrated time frame. This engaging resource provides high-interest content and vocabulary practice in context. The exercises offered in the first part of each week are simpler. As the week progresses, the activities gradually become more challenging. Likewise, the more challenging vocabulary words are offered as the year progresses.

Later sections of the book are directly related to second-grade content areas including science, mathematics, language arts, and social studies. You might plan to use these sections to complement content-area studies, bearing in mind that through repetition and repeated exposure students' vocabulary grows. It's one more way for students to practice material recently taught and for you to assess students' progress.

Daily Practice

When planning your daily routine, try one or more of these management techniques:

- Make copies of the daily vocabulary practice page for students to complete each morning. Explain to students that they should choose five of the words to create their own sentences and write them on the back of the page. Review the sentences as a whole group. Write sample sentences on the board or on a piece of chart paper.

- Distribute copies of each daily page to individual students or to small groups. You might choose to have students work together for Day One through Day Three and then individually for Days Four and Five.

- When students work independently, encourage them to exchange work with a partner and compare and discuss their answers. Or, review the correct responses together as a large group.

- Use an overhead projector or create transparencies to complete the work in a large group. Ask volunteers to help complete each item. Try completing Day One as a whole-class activity. Then have students work independently or in pairs throughout the week.

- Direct students to complete the activity pages for homework. Encourage students to share their work at home.

- Use the materials to complement content area studies. For example, you might have students conclude a lesson on the branches of government by completing the corresponding pages in the practice book.

Weekly Reviews

There is a weekly review to reinforce the work of previous days. You can use these reviews as an assessment, collecting each student's work individually. You might prefer to use the vocabulary review as an assessment tool to determine which words students still need to practice.

Monthly Reviews

At the end of each four-week set there is an activity page that reviews words taught during that month. Each monthly review includes word searches, crossword puzzles, and other engaging word games.

Extensions & Activities

Helping your students develop and build a strong vocabulary is an ongoing process. This practice book is a terrific tool to help you reach your educational goals, But it's not the only thing you can do every day to help students develop a strong vocabulary.

Use the vocabulary words in everyday speech. As you use this daily practice book make it a point to use the words in conversation. For example, instead of telling students that you are going to *show* them how to use a computer program, say that you will *demonstrate* how the program works. In this way, you are reinforcing the word, integrating it in a practical way and giving an example of how the word is used in context.

Read aloud to students. Reading aloud from authentic literature and nonfiction is an essential tool for vocabulary development. By reading aloud, you are introducing students to rich language. You can also reinforce important vocabulary words by engaging students in a book talk, focusing on words you want your students to know.

You can also create additional learning opportunities by incorporating vocabulary words into teacher-created games and activities. Here are some suggestions:

Word of the Day Challenge students to incorporate the word into their everyday speech. At the end of the day, ask students to give examples of how and when the word was used.

Synonym Concentration Have students choose five words. They should write each word and one synonym for each word on separate note cards for a total of 10 cards. Working with a partner, students should then arrange the cards face down. Students will then take turns turning over two cards at a time, trying to match the synonyms in the set. The game can also be played using antonyms.

Compound Words Write compound words on note cards, then cut the cards in half to form two separate words. Shuffle the cards, then have students put them back together to form compound words.

Super Sentences Challenge students to use the weekly vocabulary words in a sentence. Encourage them to use not just one of the words in each sentence, but several.

Homograph Art Have students expand on the list of homographs introduced in the practice book. Then have them draw pictures to go with the separate meanings for each word. Display the homographs and illustrations in class or arrange them in a class book.

Homophone Bingo Have students brainstorm a list of homophones. Then, use the words to prepare BINGO cards. Instead of calling out a letter/number combination as you would in a traditional BINGO game use one of the homophones in a sentence. Students then must identify the word in context and find its match on their BINGO board.

Nouns

1

Name ______________________

A noun names a person, place, or thing.
Circle the noun in each row.

1. wagon	came	red
2. big	small	horse
3. cold	hot	hand
4. fast	car	than
5. jump	man	try

Nouns

2

Name ______________________

A noun names a person, place, or thing.
Circle the nouns in each row.

1. A bike has two wheels.
2. The boy likes riding a horse.
3. A helmet keeps the head safe.
4. The girl sings a song.
5. The book was on the table.

Nouns

Name ____________________

3

A noun names a person, place, or thing.
Is it a noun? Write *yes* or *no* in the blanks.

1. messy ____________
2. house ____________
3. woman ____________
4. potato ____________
5. vine ____________

Nouns

Name ____________________

4

A noun names a person, place, or thing.
Draw a line to connect the nouns that belong together.

1. bakery	leaves
2. tree	desk
3. classroom	cake
4. garage	orange
5. fruit	car

Nouns

5

Name ____________________

A noun names a person, place, or thing.
Circle the nouns.

1. A man planted a garden.
2. Fruit grows on trees and bushes.
3. Bananas are a healthy snack.
4. Watch out for the hole in the ground.
5. A blanket covered the bed.

Nouns

Name ____________________

Circle the nouns.

1. Tell us the story of Johnny Appleseed.
2. Johnny Appleseed planted many seeds in the ground.
3. Apple trees grew in Pennsylvania and Ohio where he had planted seeds.
4. People picked bushels of apples from the trees.
5. People used the apples for pies and juice.

Week Two

DAILY VOCABULARY PRACTICE

Proper Nouns

Name ______________________ **1**

A proper noun names a certain person, place, or thing.
Proper nouns start with capital letters.
Underline the proper nouns.

1. Mrs. Smith visited the Oak Ledge Library.
2. Jacob wanted to go to Highcreek School.
3. The Millers went to Florida last May.
4. Sally Hughes read a book about Kwanzaa.
5. Tyrell Abbott joined the gym in Smithville.

Week Two

DAILY VOCABULARY PRACTICE

Proper Nouns

Name ______________________ **2**

A proper noun names a certain person, place, or thing.
Proper nouns start with capital letters.
Find the mistake. Write the word correctly on the line.

1. in Rockville, connecticut ____________
2. fly to Mars or pluto ____________
3. travel to norway or France ____________
4. ask sally or Pete Robbins ____________
5. lives in ohio near Indiana ____________

DAILY VOCABULARY PRACTICE

Proper Nouns

Name ______________________________ **3**

A proper noun names a certain person, place, or thing.
Proper nouns start with capital letters. Circle five proper nouns in the puzzle. Look across or down. Write them on the lines.

Word Bank
April
Mark
Monday
Sue
Tom

M	A	R	K	S
O	L	E	T	U
N	A	W	O	E
D	U	I	M	K
A	P	R	I	L
Y	J	H	O	B

DAILY VOCABULARY PRACTICE

Proper Nouns

Name ______________________________ **4**

A proper noun names a certain person, place, or thing.
Proper nouns start with capital letters.
Underline two nouns in each sentence. Write *proper* on the line if they are proper nouns.

1. The dog is chasing the cat. ____________
2. Mrs. Jones went into Crowell's Hardware Store. ____________
3. Where did Mr. Wallace find that SONY® DVD player? ____________
4. The Red Sox will play the Yankees tonight. ____________
5. Did she see the ants on her food? ____________

DAILY VOCABULARY PRACTICE

Proper Nouns

Name ______________________________ **5**

A proper noun names a certain person, place, or thing.
Proper nouns start with capital letters.
Circle the words that should begin with a capital letter.

1. The mississippi river is a great sight to see.
2. Stephanie and kevin are playing at harbor park.
3. Is bill going to california or to maine?
4. Captain rick thompson is a pilot for u.s. airways.
5. The best waiter at mama bella's pizzeria is jason.

DAILY VOCABULARY PRACTICE

Proper Nouns

Name ______________________________

Circle the proper nouns. Write them correctly on the line.

1. We will spend christmas at home. ______________
2. Can you go to the farmWay store? ______________
3. Chicago is in illinois. ______________
4. Matt's dog is an english bulldog. ______________
5. Does Jackie live on cedar street? ______________

Verbs

Name ______________________________________ **1**

A verb is a word that shows action.
Choose a verb from the word bank to complete each sentence.
Write it on the line.

1. The bird __________ to the nest.
2. She ___________ a pretty song.
3. He ___________ with a lot of tools.
4. Sara ___________ at the public pool.
5. Can you ___________ on only one foot?

flies
hop
swims
sings
works

Verbs

Name ______________________________________ **2**

A verb is a word that shows action.
Draw a line to match the words in the first column to the correct verb in the second column.

1. A dog	pops
2. Fish	shine
3. Stars	talks
4. A person	swim
5. Popcorn	barks

DAILY VOCABULARY PRACTICE

Verbs

3

Name ______________________________

A verb is a word that shows action.
Circle the verbs.

1. sing	along	collect
2. pretty	give	still
3. should	town	shout
4. crawl	carry	china
5. farmer	growl	grab

DAILY VOCABULARY PRACTICE

Verbs

4

Name ______________________________

A verb is a word that shows action.
Is it a verb? Write *yes* or *no*.

1. jump ____________________
2. tree ____________________
3. grow ____________________
4. taste ____________________
5. path ____________________

Verbs

Name ______________________________

5

A verb is a word that shows action.
Underline the verb or verbs in each sentence.

1. Ducks can walk on land and swim in the water.
2. Mary tripped as she ran to the school bus.
3. Can we visit grandmother after church?
4. Let's stay here and wait for dad.
5. He told his mother on Thursday that he felt sick.

Verbs

Name ______________________________

Circle the mistakes. Write the word correctly on the line.

1. Pandas climbs bamboo trees. ____________
2. His sister sing well. ____________
3. Flowers grows in the garden. ____________
4. My dog eat all the time. ____________
5. The boat rock in the water. ____________

DAILY VOCABULARY PRACTICE

Adverbs

1

Name ______________________________

An adverb is a word that tells about a verb. It tells how, where, or when. (He runs *quickly*. She sings *nicely*.)
Circle the adverbs.

1. He talks honestly to his friends.
2. Jon whispered quietly to Timothy.
3. The girls played happily.
4. Run quietly to the house.
5. He angrily kicked the stone.

Week Four

DAILY VOCABULARY PRACTICE

Adverbs

2

Name ______________________________

An adverb is a word that tells about a verb. It tells how, where, or when. (He runs *quickly*. She sings *nicely*.)
Does the sentence contain an adverb? Write *yes* or *no*.

1. My mother shopped slowly. ____________
2. She is a pretty girl. ____________
3. Tom walked slowly. ____________
4. Let's leave for the beach early. ____________
5. He built a castle carefully with blocks. ____________

Adverbs

3

Name ________________________________

An adverb is a word that tells about a verb. It tells how, where, or when. (He runs *quickly*. She sings *nicely*.)
Underline the adverb. Write on the line whether it tells how, when, or where.

1. Catherine lovingly hugged her baby sister. ____________
2. I often wash the dishes. ____________
3. We drove safely all the way to Maryland. ____________
4. Walk over to the park with me. ____________
5. They drove slowly. ____________

Adverbs

4

Name ________________________________

An adverb is a word that tells about a verb. It tells how, where, or when. (He runs *quickly*. She sings *nicely*.)
Underline the verbs. Circle the adverbs.

1. Joan slowly gave her report to the class.
2. He ran quickly to Mrs. Clarke's house.
3. The rain fell heavily.
4. She works daily for Mr. Keller.
5. Students chew gum loudly.

Adverbs

Name ______________________________

5

An adverb is a word that tells about a verb. It tells how, where, or when. (He runs *quickly*. She sings *nicely*.) Choose the best word. Write it on the line.

1. The boys heard the ducks quack ______________. (loudly, loud)
2. The students listened ______________. (careful , carefully)
3. I will ______________ go shopping with you. (glad, gladly)
4. Tom promised to speak ______________ to the class. (quietly, quiet)
5. The children went ______________ to the park. (happy, happily)

Adverbs

Name ______________________________

Use an adverb from the box in each sentence.

1. Brad ______________ unwrapped his gift.
2. Run ______________ into the house.
3. Did you look ______________ in the bushes for the cat?
4. Lamont ______________ planned a surprise party.
5. The band plays ______________.

secretly
quickly
happily
loudly
carefully

Monthly Review

Name ______________________________ **1**

A. Circle the nouns. Underline the proper nouns that should begin with capital letters.

1. Did you know that Pol celebrates diwali?
2. hanukkah is a Jewish holiday.
3. Some people eat potato latkes.
4. My family celebrates christmas.
5. Everyone except amy and jon eats lots of candy.

B. Find the six verbs. Look across and down.

C	H	E	W	L
L	I	G	X	E
A	D	O	C	A
P	E	A	B	P
K	N	O	C	K

chew
clap
go
hide
knock
leap

C. Circle the verb in each sentence. Underline the adverb.

1. Quietly she sang a song to the baby.
2. Bill listened carefully to the teacher's directions.
3. Tara walked slowly to the principal's office.
4. Josie nicely bowed.
5. Walk to the store quickly.

Adjectives

Name ______________________________ **1**

An adjective is a word that tells about a noun or pronoun.
It tells how many, what kind, or which one. *Pretty*, *many*, and *large* are adjectives.
Circle the adjective in each sentence.

1. The farm has a brown barn.
2. Her messy room needs to be cleaned.
3. Mom baked a huge pie for dinner.
4. Where is her spotted dog?
5. The truck made a loud noise.

Week Five

DAILY VOCABULARY PRACTICE

Adjectives

Name ______________________________ **2**

An adjective is a word that tells about a noun or pronoun.
It tells how many, what kind, or which one. *Pretty*, *many*, and *large* are adjectives.
Find the adjectives in each row.

1. small	her	long
2. dad	tall	happy
3. dog	scary	angry
4. beach	sandy	noisy
5. mean	school	kind

Adjectives

Name ______________________________ 3

An adjective is a word that tells about a noun or pronoun.
It tells how many, what kind, or which one. *Pretty*, *many*, and *large* are adjectives.
Is it an adjective? Write *yes* or *no*.

1. round ______________________
2. than ______________________
3. addition ______________________
4. silly ______________________
5. green ______________________

DAILY VOCABULARY PRACTICE
Week Five

Adjectives

Name ______________________________ 4

An adjective is a word that tells about a noun or pronoun.
It tells how many, what kind, or which one. *Pretty*, *red*, and *large* are adjectives.
Circle each adjective.

Hot weather can make people want to go swimming. It can make people want to drink cold water or lemonade. Children love to eat sweet pops in hot weather. Many children like orange pops. What is your favorite kind?

DAILY VOCABULARY PRACTICE

Adjectives

Name ______________________________

5

An adjective is a word that tells about a noun or pronoun.
It tells how many, what kind, or which one. *Pretty*, *many*, and *large* are adjectives.
Circle the adjective in each sentence.

1. The tiny girl ran to her mother.
2. Lucas was a sad boy.
3. We had a good time at the party.
4. Where is my white shirt?
5. The tall tree was old.

Week Five Review

DAILY VOCABULARY PRACTICE

Adjectives

Name ______________________________

Circle the adjectives.

1. Little kittens grow to be big cats.
2. Big elephants have floppy ears.
3. Beautiful and tall windows are on all sides.
4. The singer had a loud, strong voice.
5. Halloween can be a spooky, fun time.

DAILY VOCABULARY PRACTICE

Compound Words

1

Name ______________________________

A compound word has two words put together to make one word.
Sunshine **is a compound word made from the words** ***sun*** **and** ***shine*****.**
Write each compound word.

1. grand + father ________________
2. house + boat ________________
3. side + walk ________________
4. sand + box ________________
5. lip + stick ________________

Week Six

DAILY VOCABULARY PRACTICE

Compound Words

2

Name ______________________________

A compound word has two words put together to make one word.
Sunshine **is a compound word made from the words** ***sun*** **and** ***shine*****.**
Read each compound word. Write the two words that it is made from on the lines.

1. doghouse ____________ and ____________
2. moonlight ____________ and ____________
3. mailbox ____________ and ____________
4. bedroom ____________ and ____________
5. football ____________ and ____________

DAILY VOCABULARY PRACTICE

Compound Words

3

Name ______________________________

A compound word has two words put together to make one word. *Sunshine* is a compound word made from the words *sun* and *shine*. Match words to make a compound word. Write that word on the line.

1. under head ______________
2. eye self ______________
3. any lash ______________
4. your stand ______________
5. over where ______________

Week Six

DAILY VOCABULARY PRACTICE

Compound Words

4

Name ______________________________

A compound word has two words put together to make one word. *Sunshine* is a compound word made from the words *sun* and *shine*. Write the compound word that each phrase describes on the line.

1. a case for books ______________
2. a box for lunch ______________
3. a coat for rain ______________
4. a lace for a shoe ______________
5. a brush for paint ______________

Compound Words

5

Name ______________________________

A compound word has two words put together to make one word. *Sunshine* is a compound word made from the words *sun* and *shine*. Circle the compound word in each sentence.

1. The monarch butterfly has beautiful colors on its wings.
2. Nobody wants to go swimming while it is raining.
3. Let's play in the backyard with your dog Rover.
4. The bright moonlight is amazing to see at night.
5. I am writing a story on our class project for the school newspaper.

Compound Words

Name ______________________________

Each sentence has two words that should be put together to make a compound. Write the compound word on the line.

1. We had fun swimming under water in his pool. ______________
2. Let's go down stairs to find something to eat. ______________
3. Every one's favorite snack is popcorn. ______________
4. Finish your homework because it's almost bed time. ______________
5. This after noon I took a walk by myself. ______________

Homographs

Name ______________________________ **1**

Homographs are words that are spelled the same but have different meanings. Circle the meaning of the underlined word in each sentence.

1. The elephant drank with its trunk.	part of a tree	nose
2. Please watch where you walk here.	timepiece	look carefully
3. Don't stick me with that sharp tack!	wood	pierce
4. Try to duck below the tree branch.	move down	a bird
5. The dog's bark could be heard for miles.	part of a tree	a sound

Homographs

Name ______________________________ **2**

Homographs are words that are spelled the same but have different meanings. Draw a line from each word in the center to its two meanings.

wish for	**ball**	tall
something you chew	**bill**	sweet fruit
a dance party	**date**	skin around teeth
day or month	**gum**	round object
bird's beak	**long**	money owed

Week Seven

DAILY VOCABULARY PRACTICE

Homographs

3

Name ______________________________

Homographs are words that have the same spelling but mean different things. Write the number of the homograph next to the correct meaning.

1. I bit [1] an apple into bits [2]. ___ pieces ____ did bite
2. I can [1] lift the garbage can [2]. ___ metal container ___ am able to
3. She's fair [1] when selling fruit at the fair [2]. ___ market ___ honest
4. Use a file [1] to open the locked file [2]. ___ drawer ___ tool
5. He ground [1] up shells for the ground [2] in the garden. ___ soil ___ did grind

Week Seven

DAILY VOCABULARY PRACTICE

Homographs

4

Name ______________________________

Homographs are words that have the same spelling but mean different things. Circle the correct meaning of the underlined word.

1. Mr. Chadwick <u>left</u> school.	a direction	went away
2. She tried to <u>blow</u> the dust off.	puff	hard hit
3. Joey had to <u>duck</u> fast!	a water bird	move down
4. The class ran a <u>lap</u> in gym.	body part	one time around
5. His father worked deep in a <u>mine</u>.	tunnel	belongs to me

Homographs

Name ______________________________

5

Homographs are words that have the same spelling but have different meanings.
Draw a box around the correct meaning of the underlined word.

1. He hoped to <u>record</u> every word.	music disc	write down
2. He tried to <u>bow</u> to the princess.	hunting tool	bend down
3. Sammie <u>dove</u> into the deep pool.	did dive	a bird
4. Sara gave Jane a great <u>present</u>.	here!	gift
5. Dad found a huge <u>tear</u> in his shirt.	water from eye	a rip

Homographs

Name ______________________________

Write the letter of the correct definition next to each underlined word.

1. in <u>second</u> grade ___	a. less than a minute	b. after first
2. a sharp <u>saw</u> ___	a. a cutting tool	b. did see
3. a <u>lock</u> of hair ___	a. a door fastener	b. a curl
4. <u>bowl</u> of food ___	a. play a game	b. a round container
5. <u>down</u> to the village ___	a. a direction	b. soft feathers

DAILY VOCABULARY PRACTICE

Homophones

1

Name ______________________________

Homophones are words that sound the same but mean different things. Circle the homophones in each set of words.

1. male	mall	mail
2. eat	ate	eight
3. sea	saw	see
4. tail	tale	tell
5. tie	eye	I

DAILY VOCABULARY PRACTICE

Homophones

2

Name ______________________________

Homophones are words that sound the same but mean different things. Draw a line from a word in the first column to its homophone in the second column.

1. there	hair
2. hare	weak
3. week	one
4. won	here
5. hear	their

DAILY VOCABULARY PRACTICE

Week Eight

Homophones

Name ______________________________ **3**

Homophones are words that sound the same but mean different things. Use the correct word in the sentence.

1. You are ____________ to go to the movies.	aloud	allowed
2. The shelf was ____________ up.	high	hi
3. Where is __________ new beach ball?	hour	our
4. I __________ him to the store for milk.	sent	scent
5. Katie loves your __________ dress.	blue	blew

DAILY VOCABULARY PRACTICE

Week Eight

Homophones

Name ______________________________ **4**

Homophones are words that sound the same but mean different things. Circle the word that matches the meaning.

1. a bucket	pale	pail
2. a flower	rows	rose
3. seven days	weak	week
4. an insect	bee	be
5. a story	tale	tail

DAILY VOCABULARY PRACTICE

Homophones

5

Name ______________________________

Homophones are words that sound the same but mean different things. Write a homophone for each word.

1. dear ______________
2. hoarse ______________
3. rode ______________
4. know ______________
5. son ______________

DAILY VOCABULARY PRACTICE

Homophones

Name ______________________________

Homophones are words that sound the same but mean different things. Circle the homophone that is misspelled in each sentence. Write the correct spelling on the line.

1. Bee sure to call me tomorrow. ______________
2. My friends always due their best work in school. ______________
3. Wear are you going later today? ______________
4. Our house is built of brick and would. ______________
5. I can sea the beach. ______________

Monthly Review

2

Name ______________________________

A. Circle the mistakes. Rewrite each sentence correctly.

1. Someday I will say know to having dessert.

____

2. The sun shine is so strong we can't play ball.

____

3. I think it's grate that mom made cupcakes.

____

4. We can go to the movies oar to the playground.

____

5. Wear are you going with that popcorn?

____

B. Circle the eight adjectives from the word bank in the word find. Look across or down.

angry big busy good happy sad silly super

R	B	U	S	Y	A	S	H
S	I	L	L	Y	X	U	A
A	G	O	O	D	R	P	P
D	Q	A	W	L	R	E	P
E	B	V	A	N	G	R	Y

Prefixes

1

Name ____

A prefix is a group of letters added to the beginning of a word. A prefix changes the meaning of a word. Some prefixes are *un*– (not), *re*– (again), and *tri*– (three).
Underline the word with a prefix.

1. sing	unhappy	guess
2. redo	table	house
3. square	triangle	full
4. work	undo	stale
5. rewrite	dance	lying

Week Nine

DAILY VOCABULARY PRACTICE

Prefixes

2

Name ____

A prefix is a group of letters added to the beginning of a word. A prefix changes the meaning of a word. You see the prefix *un*– (not) in many words you meet. Add *un*– to each word. Write the new word on the line.

1. sure ____________________
2. happy ____________________
3. fit ____________________
4. broken ____________________
5. do ____________________

DAILY VOCABULARY PRACTICE

Prefixes

3

Name ______________________________

A prefix is a group of letters added to the beginning of a word. A prefix changes the meaning of the word. Some prefixes are *un*– (not), *re*– (again), and *tri*– (three). Does the word have a prefix? Write yes or no. (Sometimes a word only *looks* like it has a prefix.)

1. repaint ______________
2. uncle ______________
3. repay ______________
4. tricycle ______________
5. about ______________

DAILY VOCABULARY PRACTICE

Prefixes

4

Name ______________________________

A prefix is a group of letters added to the beginning of a word. A prefix changes the meaning of the word. Some prefixes are *un*– (not), *re*– (again), *im*– (not), *tri*– (three), and *super*– (above). Draw a line from a prefix to a word to make a new word. Write the new word on the line.

1. im	heat	1. ______________
2. over	noon	2. ______________
3. re	polite	3. ______________
4. after	cycle	4. ______________
5. tri	pay	5. ______________

Prefixes

Name ______________________________

5

A prefix is a group of letters added to the beginning of a word. A prefix changes the meaning of the word. Some prefixes are *un–* (not), *re–* (again), *im–* (not), *tri–* (three), and *mis–* (not). Write the meaning of each word on the line.

1. reappear ____________________
2. rewind ____________________
3. misbehaved ____________________
4. unable ____________________
5. impossible ____________________

Prefixes

Name ______________________________

Choose a prefix from the word bank to add to each word so the sentence makes sense. You will use one prefix twice.

1. She was _______ happy once she heard the sad news.
2. It is _______ possible for a toddler to climb a tall mountain.
3. _______ noon comes before evening.
4. Please _______ write that sloppy list of words.
5. Will you _______ pay that money I lent you?

im-
un-
re -
after-

Suffixes

Name ______________________________ **1**

A suffix is a group of letters added to the end of a word.
A suffix changes the meaning of the word. Some suffixes are –*er* (more), –*est* (most), –*ful* (full), and –*less* (without).
Circle the words that have a suffix.

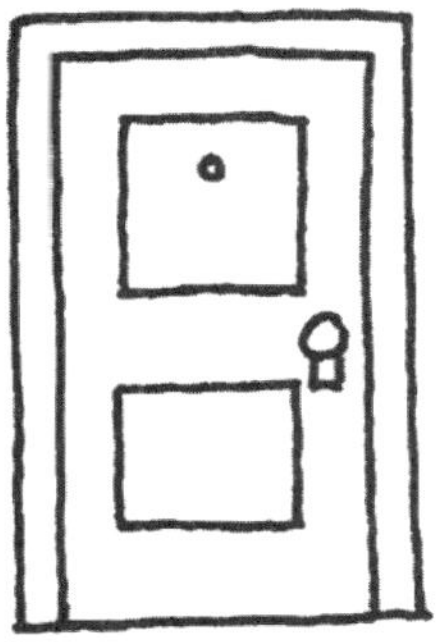

1. happiest door
2. easier big
3. sing busiest
4. bump hopeful
5. house careless

Week Ten

DAILY VOCABULARY PRACTICE

Suffixes

Name ______________________________ **2**

A suffix is a group of letters added to the end of a word. A suffix changes the meaning of the word. Adding –*ing* to a word shows that something is happening now. Adding –*ed* to a word shows that something happened in the past.
Use a word from the box to complete each sentence.

eating
making
played
walking
wished

1. Yesterday we ______________ a game.
2. We are ______________ lunch outside today.
3. I am ______________ to school this morning.
4. Last night I ______________ on a star.
5. We are ______________ cookies this morning for a snack.

Suffixes

3

Name ______________________________

A suffix is a group of letters added to the end of a word. A suffix changes the meaning of the word. Some suffixes are –*er* (more), –*est* (most), –*ful* (full), and –*less* (without).
Circle the word with a suffix in each sentence.

1. My brother is bigger than I am.
2. Rafael's joke was funnier than mine.
3. Joe's mother is always so cheerful!
4. Our dog was the smallest one at the show.
5. Who is louder, Janet or Sally?

Week Ten
DAILY VOCABULARY PRACTICE

Suffixes

4

Name ______________________________

A suffix is a group of letters added to the end of a word. A suffix changes the meaning of the word. Some suffixes are –*er* (more) –*est* (most) –*ful* (full), –less (without), and –ing (happening now). Write the meaning of each word on the line.

1. thoughtful ______________________
2. joyless ______________________
3. frightful ______________________
4. quicker ______________________
5. smartest ______________________

Suffixes

5

Name ______________________________

A suffix is a group of letters added to the end of a word. A suffix changes the meaning of the word. Some suffixes are –*er* (more), –*est* (most), –*ful* (full), –*less* (without), –*ing* (happening now) and –ed (happened in the past). Add the suffix shown to each word. Use the new word in a sentence.

1. loud + er ______________________________
2. talk + ed ______________________________
3. play + ed ______________________________
4. plant + ing ______________________________
5. home + less ______________________________

Suffixes

Name ______________________________

Use a word from the word bank to correct each suffix so it fits in the sentence. Write the corrected word on the line.

careless frightful funniest joyful smaller

1. The haunted house was frightless. ____________
2. He is the funnyed boy I have ever met. ____________
3. My cat is much smallful than yours. ____________
4. Don't be so careing with your new ball and bat. ____________
5. Her joyed laugh made everyone feel happy. ____________

Synonyms

1

Name ______________________________

Synonyms are words that have the same meaning.
Draw a line between the words that mean the same thing.

1. large	waste
2. pretty	talk
3. raise	big
4. speak	beautiful
5. garbage	lift

Synonyms

2

Name ______________________________

Synonyms are words that have the same meaning. Read each pair of words. Write *yes* if they have the same meaning. Write *no* if they do not.

1. happy	sad	____________
2. dirt	soil	____________
3. shout	yell	____________
4. help	harm	____________
5. pail	bucket	____________

Synonyms

Name ______________________________ **3**

Synonyms are words that have the same meaning.
Circle the words in each row that have the same meaning.

1. car	answer	auto
2. fountain	listen	hear
3. mean	nasty	mistake
4. wrong	yard	incorrect
5. crayon	frightened	scared

Synonyms

Name ______________________________ **4**

Synonyms are words that have the same meaning.
Choose a word from the word bank and write it on the line next to the word that has the same meaning.

1. choose ____________________
2. bright ____________________
3. brave ____________________
4. night ____________________
5. many ____________________

shiny
courageous
pick
lots
evening

Synonyms

5

Name ______________________________

Synonyms are words that have the same meaning.
Find and circle the synonyms in each sentence.

1. The stone wall was made with rocks.
2. The huge elephant ate a giant pile of hay for lunch.
3. My dad, who took me to the ball game, is a great father!
4. Sleepy Stephen was tired from the long trip.
5. Claudia was glad that Jim seemed happy with his birthday gift.

Synonyms

Name ______________________________

Read the underlined word in each sentence.
Circle the word in the next row that means the same thing.

1. The movie <u>began</u>.	tall	started	hoped
2. The <u>tiny</u> insect buzzed.	little	ugly	brave
3. Lenny's <u>pail</u> was full.	chase	bucket	flood
4. Dad was <u>angry</u> at me.	case	done	mad
5. Mrs. Bower <u>knocked</u> on the door.	kicked	banged	followed

Antonyms

1

Name ____________________

Antonyms are words that have opposite meanings.
Circle the antonyms in each row.

1. hairy	wet	bald
2. clean	dirty	full
3. early	late	yesterday
4. high	loose	tight
5. rough	tough	smooth

Antonyms

2

Name ____________________

Antonyms are words that have opposite meanings.
Write an antonym in the puzzle for each clue.

Across	Down
1. below	2. above
4. thin	3. dry
6. go	5. unkind
7. loud	6. stand

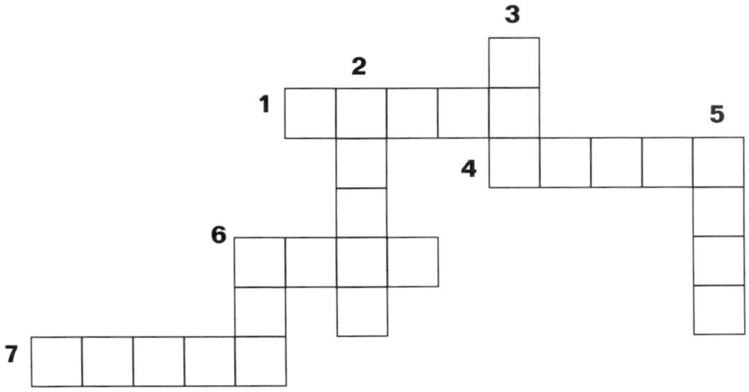

Antonyms

Name ______________________________ **3**

Antonyms are words that have opposite meanings.
Write an antonym for each word. Choose it from the word bank.

1. downstairs ______________
2. cool ______________
3. dull ______________
4. freeze ______________
5. heavy ______________

sharp
warm
light
upstairs
melt

Antonyms

Name ______________________________ **4**

Antonyms are words that have opposite meanings.
Draw lines to connect each of the antonyms.

1. sloppy	find
2. sweet	many
3. none	sour
4. scream	neat
5. lose	whisper

DAILY VOCABULARY PRACTICE

Antonyms

5

Name ______________________________

Antonyms are words that have opposite meanings.
Fill in the star if the words are antonyms.

1. begin	finish	☆
2. tame	wild	☆
3. alike	same	☆
4. sick	healthy	☆
5. gift	present	☆

DAILY VOCABULARY PRACTICE

Antonyms

Name ______________________________

Look at each set of words. Write an antonym for each underlined word.

1. small ice cream cone ____________________
2. happy circus clown ____________________
3. a road going north ____________________
4. rough wooden board ____________________
5. early winter snow ____________________

Monthly Review

3

Name ______________________________

A. Circle the mistake. Write the correct word on the line.

1. Sylvia was very rehappy with the bad news. ______________
2. If you unbehave, you will not go to the circus on Wednesday. ______________
3. She felt sick in the morning, but by the misnoon she was better. ______________
4. You should be careless when you cross the street. ______________
5. Missy is the sleepier cat I have ever seen. ______________

B. Choose a word from the word bank to complete each sentence.

antonyms afraid few hot hurry

1. *Scared* and __________________ are synonyms.
2. *Rest* and *work* are __________________.
3. Another word for *warm* would be __________________.
4. *Rush* has the same meaning as __________________.
5. *Many* is the opposite of __________________.

Letter Sounds

1

Name ______________________________

Two or more consonants that work together to make one sound are called a blend. Blends can be found at the beginning of many words. Circle the word that has a blend. Underline the blended letters.

1. trick — like
2. gate — ground
3. crash — cape
4. fool — fruit
5. wrote — wait

Letter Sounds

2

Name ______________________________

Two or more consonants that work together to make one sound are called a blend. Blends can be found at the beginning of many words. Write the correct word on each line.

1. She set the table with her best ______________.
2. A bald eagle ______________ over our campground.
3. The day was warm and ______________.
4. All the roses were in ______________.
5. We all had lemonade in tall ______________.

bloom
clear
flew
glasses
plates

Letter Sounds

3

Name ____

Two or more consonants that work together to make one sound are called a blend. Blends can be found at the beginning of many words. Underline the blend in each word. Then write a sentence using the word.

1. stone ____
2. scary ____
3. smart ____
4. snap ____
5. sweet ____

Letter Sounds

4

Name ____

Two or more consonants that work together to make one sound are called a blend. Blends can be found at the end of many words. Write *nd*, *nk*, or *nt* to complete each word. You can make more than one word with some of the blends. Write a sentence using one of the words.

1. sa ___ ___ My sentence: ______________________________
2. le ___ ___ ______________________________
3. wi ___ ___ ______________________________
4. dri ___ ___
5. ba ___ ___

DAILY VOCABULARY PRACTICE

Letter Sounds

5

Name ______________________________

Two or more consonants that work together to make one sound are called a blend. Blends can be found at the end of many words. Write *sk*, *lt*, or *st* to complete each word.

1. toa ___ ___ (breakfast food)
2. me ___ ___ (thaw)
3. ha ___ ___ (stop!)
4. de ___ ___ (school furniture)
5. sa ___ ___ (goes with pepper)

DAILY VOCABULARY PRACTICE

Letter Sounds

Name ______________________________

Circle the mistakes. Write the words correctly on the line.

1. Please klean your room. ______________
2. Don't let Jim's blaak puppy eat your toast. ______________
3. Is my desck in your classroom? ______________
4. The skary movie made me sweat. ______________
5. He used stones and klay to make the wall. ______________

DAILY VOCABULARY PRACTICE

Double-Letter Words

Name ______________________________ **1**

Double-letter words contain two of the same letter next to each other. Match the double-letter word to its meaning.

1. alley	a group of cows
2. boss	a very narrow street or path
3. cattle	one who is in charge
4. peek	to believe or think
5. suppose	look quickly

Week Fourteen

DAILY VOCABULARY PRACTICE

Double-Letter Words

Name ______________________________ **2**

Double-letter words contain two of the same letter next to each other. Write the double letter word on the line to complete each group of words.

1. ____________________ weather
2. ____________________ clown
3. ____________________ knee
4. a sharp ____________________
5. a boring ____________________

bloody
drill
silly
speech
sunny

DAILY VOCABULARY PRACTICE

Double-Letter Words

3

Name ______________________________

Double-letter words contain two of the same letter next to each other. Circle the mistakes. Then write the word correctly on the line.

1. Joan was tall and had prety hair. ________________
2. She was always in the midle of everything. ________________
3. Most of the kids were always hapy to see her. ________________
4. She liked to tell sily stories and funny jokes. ________________
5. She was wel liked by everyone in the class. ________________

Week Fourteen

DAILY VOCABULARY PRACTICE

Double-Letter Words

4

Name ______________________________

Double-letter words contain two of the same letter next to each other. Write the correct word for each sentence on the line.

bubbles   class   hammer   lessons   small

1. The ________________ boy made lots of noise.
2. I am going to take piano ________________.
3. My mother is going to a cooking ________________.
4. The carpenter swung the ________________.
5. The children had fun blowing ________________.

DAILY VOCABULARY PRACTICE

Double-Letter Words

Name ____________________

5

Double-letter words contain two of the same letter next to each other. Choose a word from the word bank to answer each question. Write it on the line.

dollar funny pillow spill wheel

1. Which word names something you rest your head on? ____________
2. Which word rhymes with *fill*? ____________
3. Which word names a kind of money? ____________
4. Which word has the same vowel sound you hear in *beetle*? ____________
5. Which word has the vowel sound you hear in *up*? ____________

DAILY VOCABULARY PRACTICE

Double-Letter Words

Name ____________________

Circle the mistakes. Write the sentence correctly on the line.

1. Please don't spil your glas of milk.

____

2. Would you pas the buter to your sister?

____

3. Our table is filed with good fods.

____

4. My brother wil not eat green beans.

____

Clipped Words

Name ______________________________ **1**

Clipped words are words that have been shortened from a longer word.
***Sub* is a clipped word for *submarine*.**
Match the clipped word to its longer word.

1. ad	automobile
2. auto	gasoline
3. bike	advertisement
4. champ	bicycle
5. gas	champion

Clipped Words

Name ______________________________ **2**

Clipped words are words that have been shortened from a longer word.
***Sub* is a clipped word for *submarine*.**
Circle the clipped word in each sentence.

1. Let's get a burger at the restaurant on the corner.
2. Please check in the fridge to see if we have butter.
3. Many scientists work in a lab.
4. Jon is a recent grad of Bellville High School.
5. Our math class will study fractions today.

DAILY VOCABULARY PRACTICE

Clipped Words

3

Name ______________________________

Clipped words are words that have been shortened from a longer word.
Sub **is a clipped word for** ***submarine*****.**
Write the clipped word for each full word.

1. telephone ____________________
2. doctor ____________________
3. graduate ____________________
4. examination ____________________
5. necktie ____________________

DAILY VOCABULARY PRACTICE

Clipped Words

4

Name ______________________________

Clipped words are words that have been shortened from a longer word.
Sub **is a clipped word for** ***submarine*****.**
Is the clipped word the correct one for each word? Write ***yes*** **or** ***no*****.**

1. submarine sub ____________
2. veteran veter ____________
3. bicycle bic ____________
4. luncheon noon ____________
5. photograph photo ____________

DAILY VOCABULARY PRACTICE

Clipped Words

5

Name ______________________________

Clipped words are words that have been shortened from a longer word.
Sub **is a clipped word for** ***submarine*****.**
Choose the correct clipped word for each sentence.

1. The basketball ________________ shouted "Foul!" three times.
   doc, ref
2. Mr. Jones needed ________________ for his mower.
   gas, subs
3. Let's get a ________________ at Dino's Grill.
   copter, burger
4. A group of ________________ were in line at the theater.
   burgers, teens
5. Jackie Robinson was a baseball ________________.
   doc, champ

Week Fifteen Review

DAILY VOCABULARY PRACTICE

Clipped Words

Name ______________________________

These sentences don't make sense. Choose a better word from the word bank to replace each underlined word.

1. The <u>taxi</u> in the paper says plants are on sale at Miller's Nursery. ________
2. I ate a sandwich at <u>champ</u>. ________
3. A line of cars waited at the <u>math</u> station. ________
4. We play basketball every week at the <u>lab</u>. ________
5. The <u>burger</u> took off straight up in the air. ________

ad
copter
gas
gym
lunch

DAILY VOCABULARY PRACTICE

Abbreviations

1

Name ________________________________

An abbreviation is a short form for a longer word. *St.* is the abbreviation of the word *Street*.
Match the word to its abbreviation.

1. Drive	Ln.
2. Lane	Hwy.
3. Highway	Rd.
4. Avenue	Dr.
5. Road	Ave.

Week Sixteen

DAILY VOCABULARY PRACTICE

Abbreviations

2

Name ________________________________

An abbreviation is a short form for a longer word. *St.* is the abbreviation for the word *Street*.
Circle seven abbreviations on this schedule.

	Mon.	Tue.	Wed.	Thurs.	Fri.
8:30 a.m.	History	Science	History	Science	History
11:30	Art	Music	Art	Music	Art
12:30 p.m.	Lunch	Lunch	Lunch	Lunch	Lunch

Abbreviations

3

Name ______________________________

An abbreviation is a short form for a longer word. *St.* is the abbreviation for the word *Street*.
Choose a word from the word bank that belongs to each abbreviation. Write it on the line.

1. Fri. ____________________
2. Sat. ____________________
3. Mon. ____________________
4. Tues. ____________________
5. Thurs. ____________________

Friday
Monday
Saturday
Thursday
Tuesday

Abbreviations

4

Name ______________________________

An abbreviation is a short form for a longer word. *St.* is the abbreviation for the word *Street*.
Choose the correct abbreviation for each sentence. Circle the correct choice.

1. Helen lives at 1001 Clay Street.	St.	Ave.
2. The postcard went to an address on Bluebird Lane.	Pl.	Ln.
3. Mary's house is on Butternut Avenue.	Ave.	Pl.
4. There are five houses on Court Place.	St.	Pl.
5. Look for the sign that says Highway 95.	Rd.	Hwy.

Week Sixteen

DAILY VOCABULARY PRACTICE

Abbreviations

Name ______________________________

5

An abbreviation is are a short form for a longer word. *St.* is the abbreviation for the word *Street.*
Write the abbreviation for each underlined word. Choose from the word bank.

1. Doctor Wells ________
2. Mister Jones ________
3. President Bond ________
4. Captain Farrell ________
5. Professor Ling ________

Capt.
Dr.
Mr.
Pres.
Prof.

Week Sixteen Review

DAILY VOCABULARY PRACTICE

Abbreviations

Name ______________________________

Write the correct abbreviation for each underlined wordon the line.

1. Tim lives on Perry Str. in the city. ________
2. Profess. Mills is the best teacher in the school. ________
3. Sara's dad works in town on Cable Aven. ________
4. Doc. Smith is Leon's dad. ________
5. Mond. is the first day of the school week. ________

Monthly Review

4

Name ______________________________

A. Add the correct double letters to the word in each sentence.

1. Will the weather be su__ __y today?
2. What are we having for di__ ___er?
3. Sue told a very si__ __y joke.
4. She was well-liked by everyone in our cla__ __.
5. Watch where you are going, or you will fall and cut your kn__ __.

B. Find the seven clipped words from the word bank in the puzzle. Look across and down.

auto
bike
gas
gym
lunch
phone
sub

S	U	B	M	Q	P
C	B	I	K	E	H
L	U	N	C	H	O
G	E	D	W	G	N
A	U	T	O	Y	E
S	J	Y	V	M	I

DAILY VOCABULARY PRACTICE

Punctuation Words

Name ______________________________ **1**

Punctuation words name the marks and signs we use in writing.
Comma **and** ***period*** **are punctuation words.**
Match the word to the symbol.

1. period	“ ”
2. comma	.
3. exclamation point	’
4. apostrophe	,
5. quotation marks	!

Week Seventeen

DAILY VOCABULARY PRACTICE

Punctuation Words

Name ______________________________ **2**

Punctuation words name the marks and signs we use in writing.
Comma **and** ***period*** **are punctuation words.**
Read the sentence. Do what each direction tells you and follow the directions below it.

Mary went to the store, the library, and the park.

1. Circle the commas.
2. Put a box around the period.

Cara asked, “Where is my jump rope?”

1. Circle the quotation marks.
2. Put a box around the question mark.

DAILY VOCABULARY PRACTICE

Punctuation Words

Name ______________________________ **3**

Punctuation words name the marks and signs we use in writing.
***Comma* and *period* are punctuation words.**
Read each sentence. Circle the word that describes the punctuation mark at the end.

1. Why are you taking that dog with you?	**exclamation point**	**question mark**
2. I am so happy to finally see you!	**exclamation point**	**question mark**
3. This is a big river.	**period**	**question mark**
4. Look out! That truck is going fast	**exclamation point**	**question mark**
5. Where can I find a playground?	**period**	**question mark**

Week Seventeen

DAILY VOCABULARY PRACTICE

Punctuation Words

Name ______________________________ **4**

Punctuation words name the marks and signs we use in writing.
***Comma* and *period* are punctuation words.**
Circle the word(s) that describes the missing punctuation mark in each sentence.

1. How are you feeling now	**period**	**question mark**
2. She bought carrots potatoes and beans.	**commas**	**exclamation point**
3. Josh said, Which one is mine?	**exclamation point**	**quotation marks**
4. We all hope she enjoys the play	**period**	**question mark**
5. I don't like blue, red or green stars	**commas**	**period**

Punctuation Words

Name ______________________________ **5**

Punctuation words name the marks and signs we use in writing.
***Comma* and *period* are punctuation words.**
Read each sentence and punctuation word that follows it. Add that punctuation to the sentence in the correct place.

1. Have a great day	**exclamation point**
2. Sam is having his birthday party soon	**period**
3. Who will help Sam celebrate his birthday	**question mark**
4. Jim said, I will help him celebrate.	**quotation marks**
5. Sam is having cake ice cream and juice.	**commas**

Punctuation Words

Name ______________________________

On the line write the name of the punctuation mark that is missing from the sentence. Add that punctuation to the sentence in the correct place.

1. Mom will be home from the store soon ______________
2. I hope she brings popcorn apples and cheese. ______________
3. Which store is her favorite grocery store ______________
4. Look, Mom bought chocolate ice cream. Yippee ______________
5. What kind of ice cream does Max like ______________

DAILY VOCABULARY PRACTICE

Week Eighteen

Contractions

Name ______________________________ **1**

A contraction is two words put together to make one shorter word. Contractions include apostrophes. *Would* and *not* are put together in the contraction *wouldn't*.
Circle the contraction in each sentence.

1. I'm having my birthday party next week.
2. It'll most likely be at my house on Saturday afternoon.
3. Jon says he's definitely going to be there.
4. Mary says she's not sure if she can come.
5. Please try to come because it'll be lots of fun!

DAILY VOCABULARY PRACTICE

Week Eighteen

Contractions

Name ______________________________ **2**

A contraction is two words put together to make one shorter word. Contractions include apostrophes. *Would* and *not* are put together in the contraction *wouldn't*.
Write the two words that make up each contraction.

1. you've ____________ + ____________
2. they'll ____________ + ____________
3. wouldn't ____________ + ____________
4. we're ____________ + ____________
5. there's ____________ + ____________

Contractions

3

Name ______________________________

A contraction is two words put together to make one shorter word. Contractions have apostrophes. *Would* and *not* are put together in the contraction *wouldn't*.
Match the two words to their correct contraction.

1. they would	won't
2. will not	we'd
3. you have	shouldn't
4. we would	they'd
5. should not	you've

Contractions

4

Name ______________________________

A contraction is two words put together to make one shorter word. Contractions include apostrophes. *Would* and *not* are put together in the contraction *wouldn't*.
Complete each contraction by adding the apostrophe in the correct place.

1. Im
2. hed
3. thats
4. youre
5. arent
6. werent
7. wasnt
8. mightve
9. youd
10. shes

Contractions

Name ______________________________

5

A contraction is two words put together to make one shorter word. Contractions include apostrophes. *Would* and *not* are put together in the contraction *wouldn't*.
Write the contraction for each sentence.

1. Our teacher ____________ (was not) in school today.
2. She ____________ (did not) feel well yesterday.
3. I wonder if ____________ (she will) go to the doctor today.
4. She ____________ (would not) go unless she was really sick.
5. We all hope ____________ (she will) be back tomorrow.

Contractions

Name ______________________________

Circle the mistakes. Write the correct contraction on the line.

1. Wel'l go camping with the Browns next weekend. ____________
2. Mom thinks the'yre the nicest family she's ever met. ____________
3. Tom said h'ed rather stay home than go out. ____________
4. Ar'ent you excited to sleep in a tent? ____________
5. No, Id' really like to sleep in my own soft bed. ____________

Book Words

Name ______________________________

1

**We use many words to talk about books and reading.
Match the book word to its meaning.**

1. cover	page that gives the book's name
2. title page	person who writes a book
3. author	person in a story
4. paperback	a book with a soft paper cover
5. character	goes on the outside of a book

Week Nineteen
DAILY VOCABULARY PRACTICE

Book Words

Name ______________________________

2

**We use many words to talk about books and reading.
Find the book word or words in each sentence.**

1. Tom went to the library to find a chapter book.
2. He looked for something by his favorite author.
3. He also needed to use the encyclopedia to learn about zebras.
4. Tom needed to use a dictionary to check his spelling.
5. The librarian also helped Tom find the books he needed.

DAILY VOCABULARY PRACTICE

Book Words

3

Name ______________________________

We use many words to describe books and the people who work with them. Choose the best word from the word bank to complete the sentence. Write it on the line.

author	chapters	pages	series	table of contents

1. She looked over the ____________ to see what was in the book.
2. The book's ____________ wrote a very funny story.
3. She has read every book in the ____________.
4. The book is divided into five ____________.
5. There are 350 ____________ in the book.

Week Nineteen

DAILY VOCABULARY PRACTICE

Book Words

4

Name ______________________________

We use many words to describe books and the people who work with them. Circle the word about books.

1. donkey	fruit	print	lick
2. brushes	cover	fuzzy	garage
3. huge	broken	mystery	moo
4. tale	pocket	neck	loose
5. bloom	doorway	bowling	pages

DAILY VOCABULARY PRACTICE

Book Words

5

Name ______________________________

We use many words to talk about books.
Is it a book word? Write *yes* or *no*.

1. pages ____________________
2. paragraphs ____________________
3. fairy tale ____________________
4. flour ____________________
5. rose ____________________

DAILY VOCABULARY PRACTICE

Book Words

Name ______________________________

Circle the word that doesn't make sense. Cross it out and write the correct word from the word bank on the line.

dictionaries	encyclopedias	librarian	pages	puzzles

1. The funny book was filled with riddles and bridges. ____________
2. The painter showed me where I could find books. ____________
3. Look in some fairy tales to find out what snakes eat. ____________
4. Mysteries list words and their meanings in ABC order. ____________
5. How many pictures did you read in that book? ____________

DAILY VOCABULARY PRACTICE

Reading and Writing Words

1

Name ______________________________

You use reading and writing words every day. They help you talk about what you read and write.
Is it a word about reading or writing? Write *yes* or *no*.

1. sentence ____________
2. letters ____________
3. gate ____________
4. poem ____________
5. report ____________

Week Twenty

DAILY VOCABULARY PRACTICE

Reading and Writing Words

2

Name ______________________________

You use words about reading and writing every day. They help you talk about what you read and write.
Unscramble the letters to make a word about reading or writing. Write it on the line.

books	draft	paper	pen	spelling

1. aeprp ____________
2. slinlpeg ____________
3. aftdr ____________
4. enp ____________
5. kobos ____________

DAILY VOCABULARY PRACTICE

Reading and Writing Words

3

Name ______________________________

You use words about reading and writing every day. They help you talk about what you read and write.
Choose the correct word. Write it on the line.

1. I do most of my writing on a ____________. (radio computer)
2. Please make sure you ____________ those words correctly. (spell flatten)
3. My little sister can make five letter ____________. (sounds vines)
4. *Card* and *hard* are words that ________________. (hum rhyme)
5. *Dark* and *light* are ________________. (synonyms antonyms)

Week Twenty

DAILY VOCABULARY PRACTICE

Reading and Writing Words

4

Name ______________________________

You use words about reading and writing every day. They help you talk about what you read and write.
Circle a reading or writing word.

1. doll	homework	brought
2. bump	gallop	pencil
3. nod	hang	draft
4. wake	vowel	trunk
5. speak	paragraph	young

DAILY VOCABULARY PRACTICE

Reading and Writing Words

5

Name ______________________________

You use words about reading and writing every day. They help you talk about what you read and write.
Choose the correct word from the word bank. Write it on the line.

letter
note
paragraph
sentence

1. A group of sentences about the same thing is a ______________________.
2. Put a period at the end of a ______________________.
3. A person's name is written with a capital ______________________.
4. Can you please write a ______________ to my teacher?

DAILY VOCABULARY PRACTICE

Reading and Writing Words

Name ______________________________

Circle the mistakes. Write the sentence correctly on the line.

1. The word *kite* has a short "i" vowel sound.
____
2. Katya wrote a thank-you report to Mrs. Green.
____
3. He read with a loud and deep finger.
____
4. If you have a good vocabulary you know a lot about trees.
____

Monthly Review

5

Name ______________________________

A. Read each sentence. Use a punctuation mark or capital letters to make each sentence correct.

1. We visited Ted's new house yesterday
2. Where is Ted living now
3. He lives on carol street near our school
4. Watch out
5. His mother gave us cookies and milk
6. Wow, your party was really fun

B. Write the contraction for each set of words. The circled letters will answer the riddle.

cannot _ (_) _' _

would have _ _ _ _ (_)' _ _

he would _ _' (_)

are not _ (_) _ _' _

you are _ _ _' _ (_)

she is _ _ _' (_)

that is _ _ _ _' (_)

What does a house wear?

_____ _____ _____ _____ _____ _____ _____

DAILY VOCABULARY PRACTICE

Science Words

Name ______________________________

1

We use many kinds of words to describe the environment. They tell about the world we live in. They name and describe the weather. They tell about the homes of animals and plants.

Read each word. Is it a word about the environment? Write *yes* or *no*.

1. sunlight ____________
2. season ____________
3. silly ____________
4. protect ____________
5. raining ____________

DAILY VOCABULARY PRACTICE

Science Words

Name ______________________________

2

We use many words to describe the world we live in. Some words tell about things that are harmful to the environment.

Circle the words in each row that tell about a problem facing Earth.

1. garbage	happy	tooth
2. bet	trash	plants
3. clue	litter	choose
4. sentence	school	waste
5. cloud	pollution	water

DAILY VOCABULARY PRACTICE

Science Words

Name ______________________ **3**

We use many kinds of words to describe the environment. They tell about the world we live in. They tell about the homes of animals and plants. Choose the correct word from the word bank and write it in the sentence.

1. The tropics are home to some huge rain ____________.
2. Coral reefs found in the ____________ are in danger.
3. It can harm the water supply when chemicals ____________ the water.
4. Worms can be helpful to the ____________.
5. Dams sometimes block the flow of ____________.

forests
ocean
pollute
rivers
soil

Week Twenty-One

DAILY VOCABULARY PRACTICE

Science Words

Name ______________________ **4**

We use many kinds of words to talk about the environment. Unscramble the letters to make words about the environment. Write them on the lines. Use the word bank for clues.

1. tcetorp ____________
2. ceudre ____________
3. evas ____________
4. trawe ____________
5. ria ____________

air
protect
reduce
save
water

DAILY VOCABULARY PRACTICE

Science Words

Name ______________________________ **5**

We use many kinds of words to describe the environment. They name and describe the weather. They tell about the homes of animals and plants. Complete each sentence with a word from the word bank.

Word Bank
Earth
habitat
protect
reuse
reduce

1. What can we do to keep ______________ clean?
2. We can ______________ useful items instead of throwing them away.
3. That way we can ______________ the amount of trash.
4. It's also important to ______________ the homes of wildlife.
5. That helps build a healthy ______________ for all of us.

DAILY VOCABULARY PRACTICE

Science Words

Name ______________________________

Read each row of words. Circle the one that does not tell about the environment.

1. reuse — cloud — box
2. cry — rain — flood
3. trash — bicycle — reduce
4. nectar — pollen — magic
5. pollution — doll — smoke

DAILY VOCABULARY PRACTICE

Science Words

Name ______________________________ **1**

We use many words to talk about Earth and its features.
Read each word. Does it tell about a feature of the Earth? Write yes or no.

1. pond ____________________
2. stream ____________________
3. parade ____________________
4. island ____________________
5. balloon ____________________

Week Twenty-Two

DAILY VOCABULARY PRACTICE

Science Words

Name ______________________________ **2**

We use many words to talk about Earth and its features.
Circle the words that tell about a feature of the Earth.

1. silly	rock	middle
2. soil	test	brace
3. final	river	mad
4. truck	ocean	hiss
5. cap	island	dream

DAILY VOCABULARY PRACTICE

Science Words

3

Name ______________________________

We use many words to describe Earth, the planet we live on. The words below are mixed up. Unscramble the letters. Write the word on the line. Use the word bank for clues.

1. elka ____________
2. eacv ____________
3. ynoacn ____________
4. dsna ____________
5. locvnao ____________

canyon
cave
lake
sand
volcano

DAILY VOCABULARY PRACTICE

Science Words

4

Name ______________________________

We use many words to describe Earth, the planet we live on. Write the word from the word bank next to its meaning.

1. wearing away at a rock ____________
2. a very dry place ____________
3. sandy land by the sea ____________
4. flat grassy land ____________
5. a higher piece of land ____________

beach
desert
hill
plain
weathering

DAILY VOCABULARY PRACTICE

Science Words

Name ______________________________ 5

We use many words to describe Earth, the planet we live on. Circle the correct word for each sentence.

1. A ______________ is very high.	beach	mountain
2. A __________across a river holds back water.	wave	dam
3. Frozen water is called ___________.	blocks	ice
4. Hot liquid rock from a volcano is ______________.	lava	pollen
5. Large bodies of salt water are ________________.	streams	oceans

DAILY VOCABULARY PRACTICE

Science Words

Name ______________________________

Circle the mistake. Write the correct word on the line.

clouds thunder water

1. The ice on the pond melted and became gas. ________________
2. The rain fell from rays in the sky. ________________
3. Lightning and measure often come together. ________________

DAILY VOCABULARY PRACTICE

Science Words

1

Name ______________________________

Many words describe our bodies and tell about being healthy. Circle the word that names a part of the body.

1. elbow garage
2. bone wind
3. crash toe
4. hope skull
5. finger idea

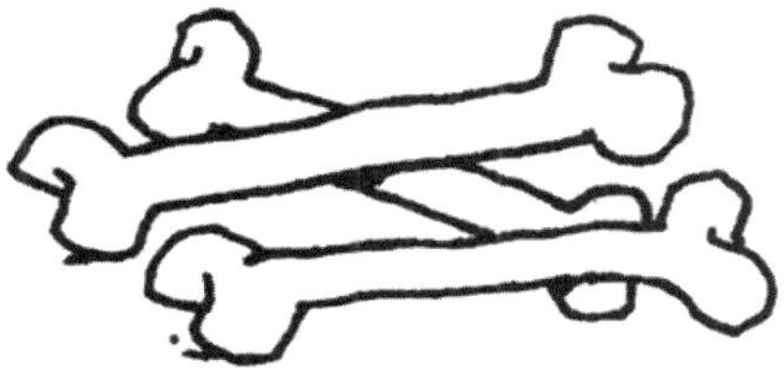

Week Twenty-Three

DAILY VOCABULARY PRACTICE

Science Words

2

Name ______________________________

Many words describe our bodies and tell about being healthy. Draw a line from the word in the first list to the word it goes with in the second list.

1. fingers mouth
2. heart hand
3. lungs feet
4. toes breathe
5. teeth pump

DAILY VOCABULARY PRACTICE

Science Words

3

Name ______________________________

Many words describe our bodies and tell about being healthy. Choose the correct word from the word bank. Write it on the line.

1. ______________ are places where sick people can get well.
2. Many ______________ work there.
3. If you feel ______________, you do not feel well.
4. Some doctors ______________ on people who need surgery.
5. You have a checkup in a doctor's ______________.

hospitals
ill
nurses
office
operate

DAILY VOCABULARY PRACTICE

Science Words

4

Name ______________________________

Many words describe our bodies and tell about being healthy. Cross out the word that is NOT a word about health or the body.

1. doctor	police	nurse
2. pills	medicine	meow
3. hospital	operation	movie
4. knee	geese	chin
5. head	twig	neck

DAILY VOCABULARY PRACTICE

Science Words

5

Name ______________________________

Many words describe our bodies and tell about being healthy. Choose the correct word. Write it on the line.

1. The ___________ mashes up the food we eat.
2. Some medicines come in the form of ___________.
3. The body needs ___________ to be healthy.
4. ___________ is not good for the body.
5. A skeleton is made up of ___________.

bones
exercise
pills
smoking
stomach

DAILY VOCABULARY PRACTICE

Science Words

Name ______________________________

Fix the mistakes. Choose a word from the word bank to correct each sentence. Write it on the line.

brain fever pumps rest throat

1. Your <u>feet</u> tells your arms and legs what to do. ________________
2. Our hearts work like <u>rulers</u>. ________________
3. Having the flu can give you a <u>laugh</u>. ________________
4. When you are sick you need lots of <u>exercise</u>. ________________
5. A cold can give you a sore <u>knee</u>. ________________

Week Twenty-Four

DAILY VOCABULARY PRACTICE

Science Words

Name ______________________________

1

Space words tell about the universe. Space words name things we see in the sky and beyond.
Are these things found in space? Write *yes* or *no*.

1. stairs ____________
2. moon ____________
3. sun ____________
4. planets ____________
5. houses ____________

Week Twenty-Four

DAILY VOCABULARY PRACTICE

Science Words

Name ______________________________

2

Space words tell about the universe. Space words name things we see in the sky and beyond. Use what you know.
Is the sentence true or not? Write *true* or *false* on the line.

1. The sun gives us heat and light. ____________
2. An astronaut flies into space. ____________
3. Astronauts fly on space shuttles. ____________
4. Planets move around the moon. ____________
5. Astronauts do experiments in space. ____________

Week Twenty-Four

DAILY VOCABULARY PRACTICE

Science Words

3

Name ____

Space words tell about the universe. Space words name things we see in the sky and beyond.
Choose the correct word from the word bank. Write it on the line.

Word Bank
crew
float
orbit
planets
space

1. A space station has been built in ______________.
2. Without gravity, astronauts can ____________ when they are in space.
3. ____________ move around the sun.
4. The word ___________ means to circle around something.
5. People who travel together on a spacecraft are the ___________.

Week Twenty-Four

DAILY VOCABULARY PRACTICE

Science Words

4

Name ____

Space words tell about what is in space. Space words name things we see in the sky and beyond.
Draw a line to match the word to its meaning.

1. explore	what an astronaut wears in space
2. astronaut	to look around or find out about
3. crater	to take off
4. launch	a scientist who goes into space
5. spacesuit	a big pit on the surface of a planet

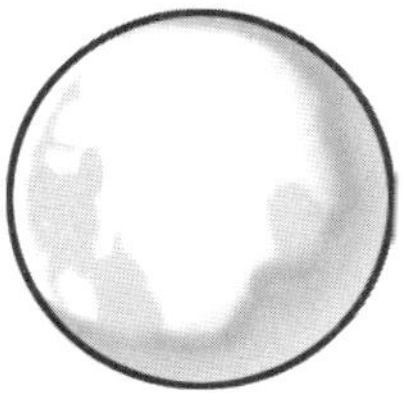

DAILY VOCABULARY PRACTICE

Science Words

5

Name ____________________

Space words name things we see in the sky and beyond. Arrange the letters to spell a word. Use the clues to help you and write it on the line.

flight shuttle stars sun telescope

1. ghtfli (a trip into space) ____________
2. copeteles (helps you see stars far away) ____________
3. ssatr (see them twinkle) ____________
4. tlutesh (flies into orbit) ____________
5. nus (huge ball of burning gas) ____________

DAILY VOCABULARY PRACTICE

Science Words

Name ____________________

Fix the mistakes. Write the correct word on the line next to each sentence.

1. Mars is a <u>sun</u>. ____________
2. Planets orbit the <u>moon</u>. ____________
3. A telescope helps you <u>fly</u> far away. ____________
4. People going into space on a shuttle are called a <u>band</u>. ____________

Monthly Review

6

Name ______________________________

A. Find the seven space words from the word bank in the puzzle. Look across and down.

astronaut crew earth moon orbit planet stars

S	T	A	R	S	D	U	N	B
D	E	P	L	A	N	E	T	O
A	S	T	R	O	N	A	U	T
R	E	S	O	A	E	M	B	R
G	E	A	R	T	H	O	F	O
T	C	R	E	W	Q	O	R	N
E	O	R	B	I	T	N	Y	A

B. Choose a word from the word bank to answer each question. Write it on the lines. The letters in circles spell the answer to a riddle!

float night planets spacesuit

1. Which word names something people can do in space? __ __ __ __ (__)
2. Which word names what astronauts wear in space? __ __ __ __ __ __ (__) __ __
3. This word is the opposite of day. (__) __ __ __ __.
4. This word names the bodies that move around the sun. __ __ __ __ (__) __ __

Riddle: Which planet likes to sing? N E P___ ___ ___ ___!

DAILY VOCABULARY PRACTICE

Math Words

1

Name ______________________________

Math words tell about working with numbers.
Circle the math word in each row.

1. count	clown	country
2. subway	subtract	submarine
3. add	apple	anything
4. ocean	office	order
5. during	difference	dandelion

Week Twenty-Five

DAILY VOCABULARY PRACTICE

Math Words

2

Name ______________________________

Math words tell about working with numbers.
Write out the number word on each line.

1. 10 ______________________
2. 15 ______________________
3. 20 ______________________
4. 9 ______________________
5. 35 ______________________

DAILY VOCABULARY PRACTICE

Math Words

3

Name ______________________________

Math words tell about working with numbers.
Draw a line from the word to the correct symbol.

1. add	$-$
2. subtract	$\times$
3. multiply	$+$
4. divide	$=$
5. equal	$\div$

Week Twenty-Five

DAILY VOCABULARY PRACTICE

Math Words

4

Name ______________________________

Math words tell about working with numbers.
Unscramble the letters to spell a math word. Write it on the line.
Use the word bank for clues.

1. piar ______________
2. tuin ______________
3. dod ______________
4. nvee ______________
5. orze ______________

Word bank:
even
odd
pair
unit
zero

DAILY VOCABULARY PRACTICE

Math Words

Name ______________________________

5

Math words tell about working with numbers.
Choose the correct word from the word bank. Write it on the line.

equal	group	less than	greater than	word

1. If two numbers are the same they are ______________.
2. Many children learn to do ______________ problems.
3. The number 6 is ______________ the number 4.
4. A set is a ______________ of things.
5. The number 5 is ______________ the number 12.

DAILY VOCABULARY PRACTICE

Math Words

Name ______________________________

Read the number problem. Write it in words instead of numbers.

1. 10 + 6 = 16 ______________________________
2. 13 – 9 = 4 ______________________________
3. 6 x 3 = 18 ______________________________
4. 0 + 14 = 14 ______________________________
5. 20 – 8 = 12 ______________________________

DAILY VOCABULARY PRACTICE

Math Words

Name ____

1

Some math words tell about geometry or the shapes of objects. Underline the geometry word in each row.

1. chirp	shape	doorway
2. square	daughter	gallop
3. ladder	fuzz	circle
4. howl	triangle	hammer
5. moonlight	side	field

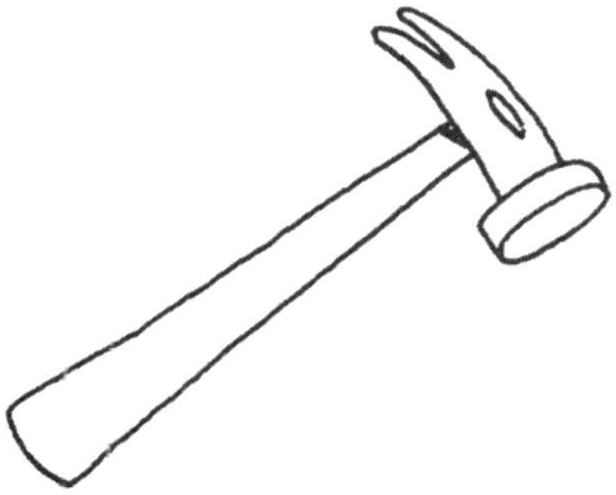

DAILY VOCABULARY PRACTICE

Math Words

Name ____

2

Some math words tell about geometry or the shapes of objects. Draw a line from the word to the correct shape.

1. rectangle 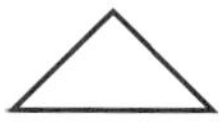

2. triangle 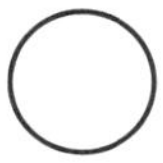

3. square 

4. circle 

5. cone 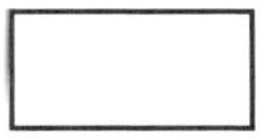

DAILY VOCABULARY PRACTICE

Math Words

Name ______________________________ **3**

Some math words tell about geometry or the shapes of objects.
Is it a geometry word? Write *yes* or *no*.

1. sides ______________
2. cube ______________
3. tomorrow ______________
4. pyramid ______________
5. bicycle ______________

DAILY VOCABULARY PRACTICE

Math Words

Name ______________________________ **4**

Some math words tell about geometry or the shapes of objects.
Choose the correct word from the word bank and write it on the line.

circle	cube	cylinder	line	triangle

1. You can draw a ______________ between two points.
2. A ______________ has no corners.
3. A ______________ has six faces.
4. A can of soup is a ______________.
5. You can easily draw a party hat by first drawing a ______________.

DAILY VOCABULARY PRACTICE

Math Words

5

Name ______________________________

Some math words tell about geometry or the shapes of objects. Draw a simple picture in the space below. Use only triangles, rectangles, squares, and circles. Then complete the sentences below.

This is a picture of ______________________. I used _______ squares, _______ rectangles, _______ triangles, and _______ circles in my picture.

DAILY VOCABULARY PRACTICE

Math Words

Name ______________________________

Fix the underlined mistake. Write the correct word on the line.

1. A <u>circle</u> has three sides. ______________
2. A square has <u>five</u> corners. ______________
3. Three rectangles have <u>six</u> sides in all. ______________
4. A cube has <u>seven</u> faces. ______________
5. Six cylinders have <u>ten</u> circles in all. ______________

DAILY VOCABULARY PRACTICE

Math Words

1

Name ______________________________

Some math words tell about measurement. They tell about size, distance, weight, and time. *Foot*, *pound*, and *hour* are measurement words.

Is it a measurement word? Write *yes* or *no*.

1. finch ____________
2. circle ____________
3. yards ____________
4. touch ____________
5. hour ____________

Week Twenty-Seven

DAILY VOCABULARY PRACTICE

Math Words

2

Name ______________________________

Some math words tell about measurement. They tell about size, distance, weight, and time. *Foot*, *pound*, and *hour* are measurement words.
Circle the measurement words.

1. frighten	ounces	knock
2. built	cattle	miles
3. minute	hose	kept
4. meter	glasses	sang
5. join	mountain	cups

Math Words

3

Name ____________________

Some math words tell about measurement. They tell about size, distance, weight, and time. *Foot*, *pound*, and *hour* are measurement words. Circle the correct measurement word.

1. I'll have two __________ of sugar in my cocoa. **bars** **teaspoons**
2. Use three __________ of butter to make the cake. **tubs** **ounces**
3. Jim drinks a __________ of milk a day. **pint** **bowl**
4. How many __________ does the car weigh? **tools** **tons**
5. It will take about a __________ to fix your bike. **week** **mile**

Math Words

4

Name ____________________

Some math words tell about measurement. They tell about size, distance, weight, and time. *Foot*, *pound*, and *hour* are measurement words.

Draw a line from the measurement word to its meaning.

1. foot	3 feet
2. yard	5,280 feet
3. mile	12 inches
4. hour	60 seconds
5. minute	60 minutes

Week Twenty-Seven

DAILY VOCABULARY PRACTICE

Math Words

Name ______________________________

5

Some math words tell about measurement. They tell about size, distance, weight, and time. *Foot*, *pound*, and *hour* are measurement words. Read each sentence. Circle the word that stands for the underlined words.

1. The ruler we used was 12 inches long.	**one yard**	**one foot**
2. The cat was in an area that was one yard wide.	**three inches**	**three feet**
3. Jerry's mother bought 16 ounces of flour.	**one pound**	**one foot**
4. It took me one hour to find to his house.	**sixty minutes**	**sixty seconds**
5. We will be away for one week in June.	**seven days**	**thirty days**

Week Twenty-Seven Review

DAILY VOCABULARY PRACTICE

Math Words

Name ______________________________

Fix the mistakes. Put the correct word from the word bank on each line.

dollars miles pounds teaspoon years

1. Carol measured the spices with a shovel. ________________
2. Our plane flew 500 inches to get to Grandma's. ________________
3. I have saved 20 buttons to buy a new CD. ________________
4. Dad used about two miles of meat in the stew. ________________
5. The ancient ship was believed to be 1,000 hours old. ________________

DAILY VOCABULARY PRACTICE

Week Twenty-Eight

Math Words

Name ____

1

Fractions name parts or sections of a whole thing. *One-fourth* and *three-eighths* are fractions. Choose the correct word from the word bank.

bottom numerator part slash

Jessica's class was learning about fractions. A fraction shows a ____________________ of something. The teacher said that fractions were written with a number on top, a number on the bottom, and a ________________between the numbers. She said the number on top is called the ______________________. The number on the _________________ is called the denominator.

DAILY VOCABULARY PRACTICE

Week Twenty-Eight

Math Words

Name ____

2

Fraction words name parts or sections of a whole thing. *One-fourth* and *three-eighths* are fractions.
Circle the word that tells about fractions.

1. airplane	numerator	believe
2. whole	certain	during
3. bump	factory	denominator
4. collect	part	ladder
5. neighbor	language	number

DAILY VOCABULARY PRACTICE

Math Words

3

Name ______________________________

Fractions name parts or sections of a whole thing. *One-fourth* and *three-eighths* are fractions.
Is it a word about fractions? Write *yes* or *no*.

1. common denominator ____________
2. fence ____________
3. fifths ____________
4. mixed number ____________
5. one third ____________

DAILY VOCABULARY PRACTICE

Math Words

4

Name ______________________________

Fractions name parts or sections of a whole thing. *One-fourth* and *three-eighths* are fractions.
Unscramble the letters. Write a fraction word on the line.

half numerator set third whole

1. ets ____________
2. lfha ____________
3. dirth ____________
4. aertumnor ____________
5. wloeh ____________

DAILY VOCABULARY PRACTICE

Math Words

Name ______________________________ **5**

Fractions name parts or sections of a whole thing. *One-fourth* and *three-eighths* are fractions.
Match the fraction word to its symbol.

1. one-eighth	1/4
2. two-tenths	3/6
3. one-half	1/8
4. three-sixths	2/10
5. one-fourth	1/2

DAILY VOCABULARY PRACTICE

Math Words

Name ______________________________

Fix the mistake in each sentence by writing the correct word on the line. Rewrite the sentence correctly.

1. The class was divided into <u>two</u> equal parts called thirds. ____________________
2. The fruit bar had three equal parts, or <u>fourths.</u> ____________________
3. The fractions 1/2 and 3/6 are <u>not equal</u>. ____________________
4. One slice from a pizza that has <u>eight</u> pieces is 1/5 of the pizza. ____________________

Monthly Review

7

Name ______________________________

A. Find the words from the word bank in the puzzle. Look across and down.

add count divide equal multiply subtract sum

J	X	C	O	U	N	T	C
S	U	M	D	S	U	J	D
G	Z	E	Q	U	A	L	I
A	S	V	Y	B	O	P	V
D	W	E	Q	T	E	R	I
D	E	N	R	R	A	E	D
I	Q	K	J	A	L	S	E
O	A	P	F	C	P	B	G
P	V	X	D	T	A	N	H
M	U	L	T	I	P	L	Y

B. Circle the mistakes. Choose a word from the word bank that will make the sentence correct. Write the word on the line.

four inches sixty three twelve

1. A yard is four feet long. ______________________
2. One ruler is twelve miles long. ______________________
3. A dozen eggs has fourteen eggs in it. ______________________
4. The number of minutes in an hour is thirty. ______________________
5. One gallon of milk is equal to three quarts. ______________________

C. Circle the geometry words.

1. The road followed a line to town.
2. Carrie made a circle on the ice in her skates.
3. The park had a baseball diamond and a playground.
4. Let's go downtown for an ice cream cone.
5. The house seemed to have corners everywhere you looked.

Week Twenty-Nine

DAILY VOCABULARY PRACTICE

Social Studies Words

Name ______________________________

1

Circle the word that is NOT something you would find on a map.

1. capital	upstairs	north
2. trail	path	bicycle
3. symbol	remember	woods
4. repair	state	country
5. ocean	whistle	east

Week Twenty-Nine

DAILY VOCABULARY PRACTICE

Social Studies Words

Name ______________________________

2

Use the correct word from the word bank in each sentence.

above   directions   globe   highways   sphere

1. A model of Earth is a ____________.
2. The shape of Earth is a ____________.
3. A map shows a place from ____________.
4. Maps can show streets, roads, and ____________.
5. A map helps you follow ____________.

DAILY VOCABULARY PRACTICE

Social Studies Words

3

Name ______________________

Complete each sentence.

blue city compass direction sign

1. Where is the Post Office in your town?
   Look at a street __________.
2. Some people live in the country; some live in a big __________.
3. North is a __________.
4. A __________ always points north.
5. On maps and globes, the color of water is usually __________.

DAILY VOCABULARY PRACTICE

Social Studies Words

4

Name ______________________

Read the clue. Write the correct map word on the lines.

seas capital west roads north

1. The opposite of east ___ ___ ___ ___
2. Another name for oceans ___ ___ ___ ___
3. The head city of a state or country ___ ___ ___ ___ ___ ___ ___
4. The opposite of south ___ ___ ___ ___ ___
5. The things cars and trucks travel on ___ ___ ___ ___ ___

Week Twenty-Nine

Social Studies Words

5

Name ______________________________

Circle the five words from the word bank in the puzzle. Look across and down.

S	N	O	R	T	H	L	W
O	K	E	A	S	T	S	E
U	H	A	G	T	W	A	S
T	A	S	T	A	T	E	T
H	C	B	N	C	A	R	K

East
North
State
South
West

Week Twenty-Nine Review

Social Studies Words

Name ______________________________

Circle the correct word.

1. Which is the ____________ to get to your town? **weigh** **way**
2. I think you should take ________ 75 to Millersville. **route** **root**
3. Does that ____________ cross Main Street? **rode** **road**
4. Yes, it crosses at the blinking ________ light. **red** **read**
5. Look for it after you pass a _______ water tower. **hi** **high**

DAILY VOCABULARY PRACTICE

Social Studies Words

1

Name ______________________________

Citizenship words tell about our government, laws, and rules. Circle the citizenship word.

1. policeman	meadow	mountain
2. broken	candle	leader
3. through	vote	weather
4. law	peek	robber
5. champ	mayor	horse

DAILY VOCABULARY PRACTICE

Social Studies Words

2

Name ______________________________

Citizenship words tell about our government, laws, and rules. Circle the correctly spelled citizenship word or words.

1. elect	elekt
2. White Houz	White House
3. president	prezedent
4. rool	rule
5. vott	vote

Social Studies Words

3

Name ______________________________

Some citizenship words tell about character and being a good citizen. Read the clue. Unscramble the letters to make a citizenship word. Write it on the line.

1. not scared avebr ____________
2. with care fulreca ____________
3. having good nessgood ____________
4. having pride roupd ____________
5. always tell the... urtht ____________

DAILY VOCABULARY PRACTICE
Week Thirty

Social Studies Words

4

Name ______________________________

Citizenship words tell about our government, laws, and rules. Underline the citizenship word or words in each sentence.

1. Our president lives in Washington, D.C.
2. He lives and works in the White House.
3. Most people try hard to obey our laws.
4. The United States is a big country.
5. Congress makes the laws of the country.

Social Studies Words

Name ______________________________ 5

Citizenship words tell about character and being a good citizen.
Use the correct word from the word bank in each sentence. Write it on the line.

fair cheat honest honor neat

1. Honest people do not ____________.
2. People in our country ____________ our flag.
3. If you follow the rules you are being ____________.
4. To tell the truth is to be ____________.
5. If you clean your room, you are being ____________.

Social Studies Words

Name ______________________________

Match the citizenship words to the meaning. Write the letter on the line.

1. the leader of our country _____
2. the capital of the United States _____
3. the first president of our country _____
4. a red, white, and blue symbol _____
5. stand for the 50 U.S. states _____

A. George Washington
B. the president
C. the U.S. flag
D. stars on U.S. flag
E. Washington, D.C.

Social Studies Words

Name ______________________________ **1**

Some words tell about culture. They describe how people live. Choose a word from the word bank to complete each sentence.

birthday
family
marry
obey
respect

1. When people grow up they often ________________.
2. How old are you? Celebrating a ________________ is a big deal for many kids.
3. In many groups of people it is important to ________________ grandparents.
4. Children learn to ________________ their parents.
5. People who are related to each other are a ______________.

Social Studies Words

Name ______________________________ **2**

Some words tell about culture. They describe how people live. Think about your life. Then read each set of words. Write something in each blank that tells about your culture or family.

1. an important holiday ______________________________
2. a language my family speaks ______________________________
3. special clothing I wear sometimes ______________________________
4. a large feast ______________________________
5. my favorite food ______________________________

DAILY VOCABULARY PRACTICE

Social Studies Words

3

Name ______________________________

Some words tell about culture. They describe how people live. Complete the sentences below with words from the word bank.

feast	Hanukkah	harvest	lights	Posadas

1. Kwanzaa celebrates the ________________ of fruits and grains.
2. At the end of Ramadan, Muslims celebrate with a tasty ________________.
3. Jewish children celebrate ________________ for eight nights.
4. Diwali is a sparkling, bright Indian festival of ________________.
5. Some Hispanic people celebrate Las ________________.

Week Thirty-One

DAILY VOCABULARY PRACTICE

Social Studies Words

4

Name ______________________________

Some words tell about culture. They describe how people live. Read each sentence. Circle the name of the holiday. Underline the words that are holiday foods.

1. I ate lots of turkey and stuffing at Thanksgiving.
2. Our Ramadan feast included chicken and fig cake.
3. During Las Posadas, we broke a piñata filled with fruits and candy.
4. My mother made special potato pancakes for Hanukkah.
5. For Kwanzaa we ate nuts and lots of fruit.

Social Studies Words

5

Name ______________________________

Some words tell about culture. They describe how people live. Find the names of family members from the word bank in the puzzle. Look across and down.

aunt brother dad grandma mom sister son uncle

D	A	D	B	R	O	T	H	E	R
A	S	I	S	T	E	R	P	Y	M
K	B	K	O	L	P	Q	R	A	O
G	R	A	N	D	M	A	T	U	M
F	K	L	M	P	Q	Z	F	N	D
T	U	N	C	L	E	B	R	T	U

Social Studies Words

Name ______________________________

Read the sentence. Find the word that describes a person in a family. Write it on the line.

1. My father taught me to play ball. ____________
2. His grandfather comes from New York. ____________
3. Mary's sister loves popcorn. ____________
4. Juan has a twin brother. ____________
5. Mei has three aunts. ____________

Food Words

1

Name ______________________________

Circle the food words.

1. garage	moonlight	cheese
2. fruit	invite	mouth
3. flood	egg	heavy
4. coyote	homework	cherry
5. sandwich	thunder	winner

Food Words

2

Name ______________________________

Write the correct word on the line.

carrot cocoa lemon pancake pizza

1. a round flat food cut into slices ______________
2. a round food served in a stack ______________
3. a sour yellow fruit ______________
4. an orange vegetable ______________
5. a hot drink ______________

Food Words

Name ______________________________ 3

Read the clue. Unscramble each food word and write it on the line.

1. breakfast food — fflewa ____________
2. this starchy food grows underground — topato ____________
3. green or baked — nbeas ____________
4. a sweet treat with syrup — pcankea ____________
5. large, green and red fruit — wamelonter ____________

Use one word from above in a sentence about food.

____

Food Words

Name ______________________________ 4

Circle the correct food word.

1. Mrs. Miller gave Tom and me a ____________. **cooky, cookie**
2. We ate corn, beans, and hamburgers at the ____________. **piknic, picnic**
3. We were so hungry we stopped to have ____________ and cheese. **crackers, crakers**
4. His favorite snack is crisp ____________. **fruut, fruit**
5. We went to a ____________ for breakfast. **diner, dinner**

DAILY VOCABULARY PRACTICE

Food Words

5

Name ______________________________

Choose a word from the word bank that means about the same as the underlined words.

cake dinner knife peas plate

1. They had a big meal in the evening. ______________
2. He cut his meat with a tool. ______________
3. His food was eaten from a round dish. ______________
4. He ate chicken and little round green vegetables. ______________
5. Then he had a piece of a sweet dessert. ______________

DAILY VOCABULARY PRACTICE

Food Words

Name ______________________________

Find the mistake. Write the correct word on the line.

1. She set the table with her best dishus. ______________
2. Will you bake or fry that chickin? ______________
3. Mom made a huge pumken pie for Thanksgiving. ______________
4. We had holiday cookies with sprinkels. ______________
5. At Joe's house we drank the best berri juice. ______________

Monthly Review

Name ______________________________ **8**

A. Read each sentence. Write the missing word in the puzzle.

Across

1. The president lives in the __________ __________.
5. Rules for our country are called __________.
6. The United States is a __________.

Down

2. The president's wife is called the __________ Lady.
3. People __________ to choose a president.
4. The president meets with __________ from other countries.

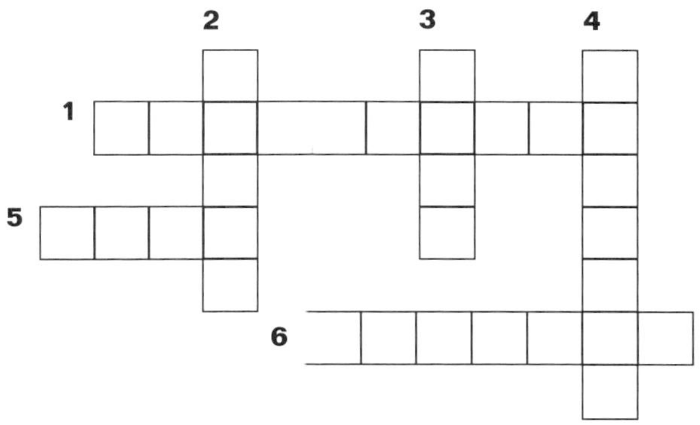

country
first
laws
leaders
vote
White House

B. Complete the sentence with the correct word from the word bank.

branches citizens country president stars

1. George Washington was our first ____________________.
2. The people of our country are called ____________________.
3. The United States has three ____________________ of government.
4. Our flag is a symbol of our ____________________.
5. The United States flag has 50 ____________________.

Transportation Words

1

Name ______________________________

Is it a word that tells about transportation? Write *yes* or *no*.

1. highway ____________________
2. bicycle ____________________
3. cereal ____________________
4. railroad ____________________
5. cares ____________________

Transportation Words

2

Name ______________________________

Complete the sentences with the correct word from the word bank.

airports bicycle tracks traffic truck

1. A ________________ carries goods to market.
2. A passenger train travels on ________________.
3. A highway slowdown is a ________________ jam.
4. Up, up and away! Planes take off from ________________.
5. A ________________ moves by foot power.

DAILY VOCABULARY PRACTICE

Transportation Words

3

Name ______________________________

Match the vehicle with what powers it.

1. sailboat	gasoline
2. car	jet fuel
3. subway	muscles
4. rowboat	electricity
5. airplane	wind

Week Thirty-Three

DAILY VOCABULARY PRACTICE

Transportation Words

4

Name ______________________________

Match the vehicle with its home.

automobile	station
train	airport
helicopter	dock
sailboat	garage
jet	heliport

DAILY VOCABULARY PRACTICE

Transportation Words

5

Name ______________________________

Circle the transportation words in each sentence.

1. Jan took the school bus home from school.
2. The subway was running late.
3. We took a taxi to the airport.
4. The train stopped at the station.
5. The sailboat turned into the wind.

DAILY VOCABULARY PRACTICE

Transportation Words

Name ______________________________

Complete the story with the transportation words from the word bank.

What a great trip! A ____________ driver took us to the railroad ____________. There we boarded a ____________ to the city. An underground ____________ train took us to the ____________. There we caught an airplane.

Word bank:
- airport
- station
- subway
- taxi
- train

DAILY VOCABULARY PRACTICE

School Words

1

Name ______________________________

We use many words to describe and talk about school.
Is it a school word? Write *yes* or *no*.

1. teacher ____________
2. student ____________
3. born ____________
4. books ____________
5. dogs ____________

Week Thirty-Four

DAILY VOCABULARY PRACTICE

School Words

2

Name ______________________________

We use many words to describe and talk about school.
Match the school word to its meaning.

1. ___ something you write with — A. classroom
2. ___ someone who teaches — B. principal
3. ___ person in charge of a school — C. pencil
4. ___ person who helps you find a book to read — D. teacher
5. ___ where you go to learn — E. librarian

School Words

3

Name ______________________________

We use many words to describe and talk about school.
Circle the school word in each sentence.

1. The crossing guard waved her stop sign.
2. We almost missed the school bus.
3. The principal's office was bright and sunny.
4. We ate pizza and drank juice in the cafeteria.
5. The students ran out to the playground.

School Words

4

Name ______________________________

We use many words to describe and talk about school.
Choose a word from the word box to answer each question.

chalk   gym   read   ruler   workbook

1. Which word rhymes with *walk*? ____________
2. Which word has the same vowel sound you hear in *meal*? ____________
3. Which word is a compound word? ____________
4. Which word names a sports room? ____________
5. Which word names a measuring stick? ____________

DAILY VOCABULARY PRACTICE

School Words

Name ______________________

5

We use many kinds of words to describe and talk about school. Complete these compound words.

1. ______________ board
2. ______________ room
3. play ______________
4. class ______________
5. ______________ pack

back
chalk
ground
lunch
room

DAILY VOCABULARY PRACTICE

School Words

Name ______________________

Write a short sentence using each school word.

1. teacher ______________________
2. cafeteria ______________________
3. pencil ______________________
4. principal ______________________
5. bus driver ______________________

Sound Words

1

Name ______________________________

Sound words describe a sound. *Bam* and *zonk* are sound words. Circle the sound word.

1. basket	click	watch
2. never	seat	fizz
3. answer	dance	bowwow
4. buzz	bedroom	careful
5. fence	swish	hope

Week Thirty-Five

DAILY VOCABULARY PRACTICE

Sound Words

2

Name ______________________________

Sound words describe a sound. *Bam* and *zonk* are sound words. Circle the word that rhymes with the sound word.

1. **hoot**	movie	boot
2. **blink**	sink	toe
3. **woof**	hidden	hoof
4. **hiss**	miss	choose
5. **moan**	joke	loan

Sound Words

3

Name ______________________________

Sound words describe a sound. *Bam* and *zonk* are sound words. Circle the sound words.

1. A squeak in the wall scared the young girl.
2. His boots crunched on the hard icy snow.
3. The snake gave a soft hiss and moved away.
4. Smack! The bat hit the ball and sent it flying.
5. Crackle, crackle, pop! The logs burned brightly in the fire.

DAILY VOCABULARY PRACTICE
Week Thirty-Five

Sound Words

4

Name ______________________________

Sound words describe a sound. *Bam* and *zonk* are sound words. Write the correct word from the word box in each sentence.

growl moo neigh oink pounding

1. A pig will ________________.
2. A bear can ________________.
3. The horse began to ________________.
4. A cow likes to ________________.
5. The horse's feet made a ________________ sound.

DAILY VOCABULARY PRACTICE

Sound Words

5

Name ______________________________

Sound words describe a sound. *Bam* and *zonk* are sound words. Underline the correct sound word.

1. The dog ____________ all day at the cars and trucks.
   barked **barkked**
2. The wolf ______________ to the others in its pack.
   howled **houled**
3. The children all ____________ at the clown.
   gigled **giggled**
4. The old owl had a loud ____________ that it used each night.
   hute **hoot**
5. Her boots _____________ in the barnyard mud.
   sqwished **squished**

DAILY VOCABULARY PRACTICE

Sound Words

Name ______________________________

Read the clue. Spell the sound word on the lines.

1. sound of a duck ___ ___ ___ ___ ___
2. what a sheep says ___ ___ ___
3. what an owl does ___ ___ ___ ___
4. a happy kitten's sound ___ ___ ___ ___
5. the noise of a bell ___ ___ ___ ___

Week Thirty-Six

DAILY VOCABULARY PRACTICE

Sports Words

Name ______________________________ 1

Underline the sports word.

1. tea	team	stuff
2. wife	welcome	winner
3. flour	finger	finish
4. bump	bunch	ball
5. scare	score	scientist

Week Thirty-Six

DAILY VOCABULARY PRACTICE

Sports Words

Name ______________________________ 2

Choose a sports word from the word bank to complete each sentence.

baseball   basketball   forward   score   soccer

1. The ________________ game was played on the diamond in town.
2. Where are the ________________ balls?
3. Jon plays the ________________ position on the city team.
4. The ________________ court is next to the gym.
5. The final ________________ was 61 to 45.

Sports Words

Name ______________________________ 3

Circle the correct spelling of each sports word.

1. right field   rite field
2. hoom plate   home plate
3. captun   captain
4. catcher   katcher
5. goaly   goalie

Sports Words

Name ______________________________ 4

Write the correct sports word on the line to complete the sentence.

1. Tom took first ___________ in the track meet.

   place   **plate**

2. He put on his ___________ for the football game.

   helmet   **ice skates**

3. The player's kick sent the ___________ flying into the air.

   football   **baseball**

4. Sophie's dad taught her to catch a baseball with her ___________.

   goal   **glove**

Sports Words

Name ______________________ **5**

Add the suffix *-er* to each word to make the names of people in sports. Write the word on the line.

1. catch ______________
2. pitch ______________
3. boat ______________
4. climb ______________
5. jump ______________

Choose one of the words to use in a sentence. Write it here.

____

Sports Words

Name ______________________

Find the mistake. Write the correct word on the line.

1. Why does a boxer need to use gluves? ______________
2. The player kicked the ball down the feeld. ______________
3. The baseball teem was in good shape to play the game. ______________
4. The strong bater sent the ball over the fence. ______________
5. Where are the ice scates you gave me last year? ______________

Monthly Review

9

Name ____

A. Circle the nine sports words from the word bank in the puzzle. Look across and down.

baseball football goal lose run score soccer track win

B	A	S	E	B	A	L	L
G	O	C	H	R	U	N	O
O	S	O	C	C	E	R	S
A	B	R	W	I	N	T	E
L	A	E	T	R	A	C	K
F	O	O	T	B	A	L	L

B. Unscramble the letters to make a sports word. Use the clues to help you.

1. nwi ____ ____ ____ (opposite of lose)
2. oachc ___ ___ ___ ___ ___ (someone who helps)
3. amte____ ___ ___ ____ (the group that plays)
4. lfou ___ ___ ____ ____ (mistake)
5. oresc ___ __ ___ ___ ___ (goal!)

C. Read the clue. Write the sports word on the line.

1. Something that is played; it rhymes with *same* ____________
2. It is kicked or batted; starts with *b* ____________
3. The score in baseball; starts with *r* ____________
4. A group of players; rhymes with *seam* ____________
5. Name of a sport; rhymes with *snack* ____________

Daily Vocabulary Practice

Answers — Grade 2

Week 1

Day 1

1. wagon 2. horse 3. hand 4. car 5. man

Day 2

1. bike, wheels 2. boy, horse 3. helmet, head 4. girl, song 5. book, table

Day 3

1. no 2. yes 3. yes 4. yes 5. yes

Day 4

1. bakery – cake 2. tree – leaves 3. classroom – desk 4. garage – car 5. fruit – orange

Day 5

1. man, garden 2. fruit, trees, bushes 3. bananas, snack 4. hole, ground 5. blanket, bed

Review

1. story, Johnny Appleseed 2. Johnny Appleseed, seeds, ground 3. apple trees, Pennsylvania, Ohio, seeds 4. people, bushels, apples, trees 5. people, apples, pies, juice

Week 2

Day 1

1. Mrs. Smith, Oak Ledge Library 2. Jacob, Highcreek School 3. Millers, Florida, May 4. Sally Hughes, Kwanzaa 5. Tyrell Abbott, Smithville

Day 2

1. Rockville, Connecticut 2. Mars Pluto 3. Norway France 4. Sally Pete Robbins 5.Ohio Indiana

Day 3

M	A	R	K	S
O	L	E	T	U
N	A	W	O	E
D	U	I	M	K
A	P	R	I	L
Y	J	H	O	B

Day 4

1. dog, cat 2. Mrs. Jones, Crowell's Hardware Store, proper 3. Mr. Wallace, SONY DVD, proper 4. Red Sox, Yankees, proper 5. ants, food

Day 5

1. Mississippi River 2. Kevin, Harbor Park 3. Bill, California, Maine 4. Rick Thompson, U.S. Airways 5. Mama Bella's Pizzeria, Jason

Review

1. Christmas 2. Farmway 3. Illinois 4. English Bulldog 5. Cedar Street

Week 3

Day 1

1. flies 2. sings 3. works 4. swims 5. hop

Day 2

1. A dog – barks 2. Fish – swim 3. Stars – shine 4. A person – talks 5. Popcorn – pops

Day 3

1. sing, collect 2. give 3. should shout 4. crawl, carry 5. growl, grab

Day 4

1. yes 2. no 3. yes 4. yes 5. no

Day 5

1. walk, swim 2. tripped, ran, 3. visit 4. stay, wait 5. told, felt

Review

1. climb 2. sings 3. grow 4. eats 5. rocks

Week 4

Day 1

1. honestly 2. quietly 3. happily 4. quietly 5. angrily

Day 2

1. yes 2. no 3. yes 4. yes 5. yes

Day 3

1. lovingly, how 2. often, when 3. safely, how 4. over, where 5. slowly, how

Day 4

1. gave, slowly 2. ran, quickly 3. fell, heavily 4. works, daily 5. chew, loudly

Day 5

1. loudly 2. carefully 3. gladly 4. quietly 5. happily

Review

1. happily 2. quickly 3. carefully 4. secretly 5. loudly

Month 1 Review

A. 1. Pol, Diwali 2. Hanukkah holiday 3. people, latkes 4. family, Christmas 5. Amy, Jon, candy

B.

C	H	E	W	L
L	I	G	X	E
A	D	O	C	A
P	E	A	B	P
K	N	O	C	K

C. 1. sang, quietly 2. listened, carefully 3. walked, slowly 4. bowed, nicely 5. walk, quickly

Week 5

Day 1

1 brown 2. messy 3. huge 4 spotted 5. loud

Day 2

1. small, long 2. tall, happy 3. scary, angry 4. sandy, noisy 5. mean, kind

Day 3

1. yes 2. no 3. no 4. yes 5. yes

Day 4

Hot, cold, sweet, hot, orange, favorite

Day 5

1. tiny, 2. sad, 3. good, 4. white, 5. tall

Review

1. little, big 2. big, floppy 3. beautiful, tall all 4. loud, strong 5. spooky, fun

Week 6

Day 1

1. grandfather 2. houseboat 3. sidewalk 4. sandbox 5. lipstick

Day 2

1. dog, house 2. moon, light 3. mail, box 4. bed, room 5. foot, ball

Day 3

1. understand 2. eyelash 3. anywhere 4. yourself 5. overhead

Day 4

1. bookcase 2. lunchbox 3. raincoat 4. shoelace 5. paintbrush

Day 5
1. butterfly 2. nobody 3. backyard 4. moonlight 5. newspaper

Review
1. underwater 2. downstairs, 3. everyone's 4. bedtime 5. afternoon,

Week 7
Day 1
1. nose 2. look carefully 3. pierce 4. move down 5. a sound

Day 2
1. ball – dance party, round object 2. bill – bird's beak, money owed 3. date – sweet fruit, day or month 4. gum – tissue around teeth, something you chew 5. long – tall, wish for

Day 3
1. 2 – pieces, 1 – did bite 2. 2 – metal container, 1 – am able to 3. 2 – market 1 – honest 4. 2 – drawer 1 – tool 5. 2 – soil 1 – did grind

Day 4
1. went away 2. puff 3. move down 4. one time around 5. tunnel

Day 5
1. write down 2. bend down 3. did dive 4. gift 5. a rip

Review
1. b 2. a 3. b 4. b 5 a

Week 8
Day 1
1. male, mail 2. ate, eight 3. sea, see 4. tail, tale 5. eye, I

Day 2
1. there – their 2. hare – hair 3. week – weak 4. won – one 5. hear – here

Day 3
1. allowed 2. high 3. our 4. sent 5. blue

Day 4
1. pail 2. rose 3. week 4. bee 5. tale

Day 5
1. deer 2. horse 3. road 4. no 5. sun

Review
1. be 2. do 3. where 4. wood 5. see

Month 2 Review
A 1. Someday I will say no to having dessert. 2. The sunshine is so strong we can't play ball. 3. I think it's great that mom made cupcakes. 4. We can go to the movies or to the playground. 5. Where are you going with that popcorn?

B.
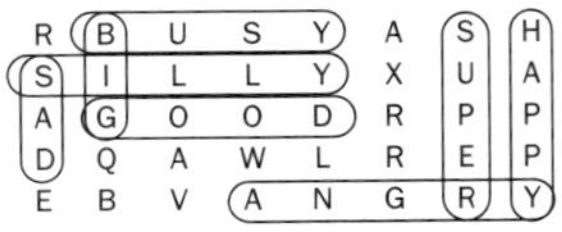

Week 9
Day 1
1. unhappy 2. redo 3. triangle 4. undo 5. rewrite

Day 2
1. unsure 2. unhappy 3. unfit 4. unbroken 5. undo

Day 3
1. yes 2. no 3. yes 4. yes 5. no

Day 4
1. im – polite 2. over – heat 3. re – pay 4. after – noon 5. tri – cycle

Day 5
1. appear again 2. wind again 3. did not behave 4. not able 5. not possible

Review

1. un- 2. im- 3. after- 4. re- 5. re-

Week 10
Day 1
1. happiest 2. easier 3. busiest 4. hopeful 5. careless

Day 2
1. played 2. eating 3. walking 4. wished 5. making

Day 3
1. bigger 2. funnier 3. cheerful 4. smallest 5. louder

Day 4
1. full of thought 2. without joy 3. full of fright 4. with more speed 5. the most smart

Day 5
1. louder 2. talked 3. played 4. planting 5. homeless Answers will vary

Review
1. frightful 2. funniest 3. smaller 4. careless 5. joyful

Week 11
Day 1
1. large – big 2. pretty – beautiful 3. raise – lift 4. speak – talk 5. garbage – waste

Day 2
1. no 2. yes 3. yes 4. no 5. yes

Day 3
1. car, auto 2. listen, hear 3. mean, nasty 4. wrong, incorrect 5. frightened, scared

Day 4
1. pick 2. shiny 3. courageous 4. evening 5. lots

Day 5
1. stone, rocks 2. huge, giant 3. dad, father 4. sleepy, tired 5. glad, happy

Review
1. started 2. little 3. bucket 4. mad 5. banged

Week 12
Day 1
1. hairy, bald 2. clean, dirty 3. early, late 4. loose, tight 5. rough, smooth

Day 2
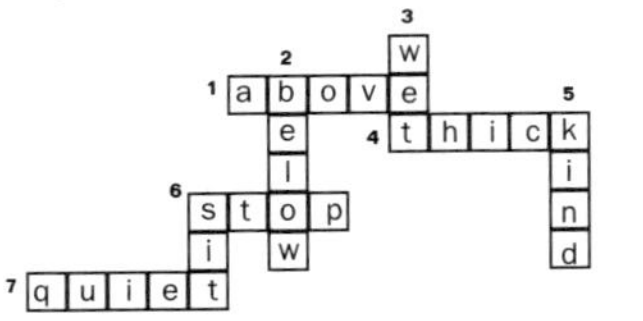

Day 3
1. upstairs 2. warm 3. sharp 4. melt 5. light

Day 4
1. sloppy – neat 2. sweet – sour 3. none – many 4. scream – whisper 5. lose – find

Day 5
1. fill in star 2. fill in star 3. leave blank 4. fill in star 5. leave blank

Review
1. big 2. sad 3. south 4. smooth 5. late

Month 3 Review
A 1. unhappy 2. misbehave 3. afternoon 4. careful 5. sleepiest

B 1. afraid 2. antonyms 3. hot 4. hurry 5. few

Week 13
Day 1
1. trick 2. ground 3. crash 4. fruit 5. wrote

Day 2
1. plates 2. flew 3. clear 4. bloom 5. glasses

Day 3

any sentence using the correct word

1. stone 2. scary 3. smart 4. snap 5. sweet

Day 4

any sentence using the correct word

1. sand 2. lent 3. wink 4. drink 5. band

Day 5

1. toast 2. melt 3. halt 4. desk 5. salt

Review

1. klean – clean 2. blaak – black 3. desck – desk 4. skary – scary 5. klay – clay

Week 14

Day 1

1. alley – a very narrow street or path 2. boss – one who is in charge 3. cattle – a group of cows 4. peek – look quickly 5. suppose – to believe or think

Day 2

1. sunny 2. silly 3. bloody 4. drill 5. speech

Day 3

1. pretty 2. middle 3. happy 4. silly 5. well

Day 4

1. small 2. lessons 3. class 4. hammer 5. bubbles

Day 5

1. pillow 2. spill 3. dollar 4. wheel 5. funny

Review

1. Please don't spill your glass of milk. 2. Would you pass the butter to your sister? 3. Our table is filled with good foods. 4. My brother will not eat green beans.

Week 15

Day 1

1. ad – advertisement 2. auto – automobile 3. bike – bicycle 4. champ – champion 5. gas – gasoline

Day 2

1. burger 2. fridge 3. lab 4. grad 5. math

Day 3

1. phone 2. doc 3. grad 4. exam 5. tie

Day 4

1. yes 2. no 3. no 4. no 5. yes

Day 5

1. ref 2. gas 3. burger 4. teens 5. champ

Review

1. ad 2. lunch 3. gas 4. gym 5. copter

Week 16

Day 1

1. Drive – Dr. 2. Lane – Ln. 3. Highway – Hwy. 4. Avenue – Ave. 5. Road – Rd.

Day 2

a.m., p.m., Mon. Tue, Wed, Thurs, Fri

Day 3

1. Friday 2. Saturday 3. Monday 4. Tuesday 5. Thursday

Day 4

1. St. 2. Ln. 3. Ave. 4. Pl. 5. Hwy.

Day 5

1. Dr. 2. Mr. 3. Pres. 4. Capt. 5. Prof.

Review

1. St. 2. Prof. 3. Ave. 4. Dr. 5. Mon.

Month 4 Review

A 1. sunny 2. dinner 3. silly 4. class 5. knee

B.

S	U	B	M	Q	P
C	B	I	K	E	H
L	U	N	C	H	O
G	E	D	W	G	N
A	U	T	O	Y	E
S	J	Y	V	M	I

Week 17

Day 1

1. period **.** 2. comma **,** 3. exclamation point **!** 4. apostrophe **'** 5. quotation marks **" "**

Day 2

1. Mary went to the store(,) the library(,) and the park[.] 2. Cara asked, (")Where is my jump rope[?](")

Day 3

1. question mark 2. exclamation point 3. period 4. exclamation mark 5. question mark

Day 4

1. question mark 2. commas 3. quotation marks 4. period 5. period

Day 5

1. Have a great day.
2. Sam is having his birthday soon.
3. Who will help Sam celebrate his birthday? 4. Jim said, "I will help him celebrate." 5. Sam is having cake, ice cream, and juice.

Review

1. period – Mom will be home from the store soon. 2. commas – I hope she brings popcorn, apples, and cheese. 3. question mark – Which store is her favorite grocery store? 4. exclamation mark – Look, Mom bough chocolate ice cream! Yippee! 5. question mark – What kind of ice cream does Max like?

Week 18

Day 1

1. I'm 2. It'll 3. he's 4. she's 5. it'll

Day 2

1. you have 2. they will 3. would not 4. we are 5. there is

Day 3

1. they would – they'd 2. will not – won't 3. you have – you've 4. we would – we'd 5. should not – shouldn't

Day 4

1. I'm 2. he'd 3. that's 4. you're 5. aren't 6. weren't 7. wasn't 8. might've 9. you'd 10. she's

Day 5

1. wasn't 2. didn't 3. she'll 4. wouldn't 5. she'll

Review

1. Wel'l – We'll 2. the'yre – they're 3. h'ed – he'd 4. ar'ent – aren't 5. Id' – I'd

Week 19

Day 1

1. cover – goes on the outside of a book 2. title page – page that gives the book's name 3. author – person who writes a book 4. paperback – a book with a soft paper cover 5. character – person in a story.

Day 2

1. library, chapter book 2. author 3. encyclopedia 4. dictionary, spelling 5. librarian books.

Day 3

1. Table of Contents 2. author 3. series 4. chapters 5. pages

Day 4

1. print 2. cover 3. mystery 4. tale 5. pages

Day 5

1. yes 2. yes 3. yes 4. no 5. no

Review

1. puzzles 2. librarian 3. encyclopedias 4. dictionaries 5. pages

Week 20

Day 1

1. yes 2. yes 3. no 4. yes 5. yes

Day 2

1. paper 2. spelling 3. draft 4. pen 5. books

Day 3

1. computer 2. spell 3. sounds 4. rhyme 5. antonyms

Day 4

1. homework 2. pencil 3. draft 4. vowel 5. paragraph

Day 5

1. paragraph 2. sentence 3. letter 4. note

Review

1. The word "kite" has a long i vowel sound. 2. Katya wrote a thank-you note to Mrs. Green. 3. He read with a loud and deep voice. 4. If you have a good vocabulary you know a lot about words.

Month 5 Review

A 1. We visited Ted's new house yesterday. 2. Where is Ted living now? 3. He lives on Carol Street near our school. 4. Watch out! 5. His mother gave us cookies and milk.

6. Wow, your party was really fun!

B 1.

cannot	_ (A) _' _
would have	_ _ _ _ (D)' _ _
he would	_ _' (D)
are not	_ (R) _ _' _
you are	_ _ _' _ (E)
she is	_ _ _' (S)
that is	_ _ _ _' (S)

Week 21

Day 1

1. yes 2. yes 3. no 4. yes 5. yes

Day 2

1. garbage 2. trash 3. litter 4. waste 5. pollution

Day 3

1. forests 2. ocean 3. pollute 4. soil 5. rivers

Day 4

1. protect 2. reduce 3. save 4. water 5. air

Day 5

1. Earth 2. reuse 3. reduce 4. protect 5. habitat

Review

1. box 2. cry 3. bicycle 4. magic 5. doll

Week 22

Day 1

1. yes 2. yes 3. no 4. yes 5. no

Day 2

1. rock 2. soil 3. river 4. ocean 5. island

Day 3

1. lake 2. cave 3. canyon 4. sand 5. volcano

Day 4

1. weathering 2. desert 3. beach 4. plain 5. hill

Day 5

1. mountain 2. dam 3. ice 4. lava 5. oceans

Review

1. water 2. clouds 3. thunder

Week 23

Day 1

1. elbow 2. bone 3. toe 4. skull 5. finger

Day 2

1. fingers – hand 2. heart – pump 3. lungs – breathe 4. toes – feet 5. mouth – teeth

Day 3

1. hospitals 2. nurses 3. ill 4. operate 5. office

Day 4

1. police 2. meow 3. movie 4. geese 5. twig

Day 5

1. stomach 2. pills 3. exercise 4. smoking 5. bones

Review

1. brain 2. pumps 3. fever 4. rest 5. throat

Week 24

Day 1

1. no 2. yes 3. yes 4. yes 5. no

Day 2

1. yes 2. yes 3. yes 4. no 5. yes

Day 3

1. space 2. float 3. planets 4. orbit 5. crew

Day 4

1. explore – to look around or find out about 2. astronaut – a scientist who goes into space 3. crater – a big pit on the surface of a planet 4. launch – to lift or take off 5. spacesuit – what an astronaut wears in space

Day 5

1. flight 2. telescope 3. stars 4. shuttle 5. sun

Review

1. Mars is a planet. 2. Planets orbit the Sun. 3. A telescope helps you see far away. 4. People going into space on a shuttle are called a crew.

Month 6 Review

A.

S	T	A	R	S	D	U	N	B
D	E	P	L	A	N	E	T	O
A	S	T	R	O	N	A	U	T
R	E	S	O	A	E	M	B	R
G	E	A	R	T	H	O	F	O
T	C	R	E	W	Q	O	R	N
E	O	R	B	I	T	N	Y	A

B 1. float 2. spacesuit 3. night 4. planets Neptune

Week 25

Day 1

1. count 2. subtract 3. add 4. order 5. difference

Day 2

1. ten 2. fifteen 3. twenty 4. nine 5. thirty-five

Day 3

1. add + 2. subtract – 3. multiply x 4. divide ÷ 5. equal =

Day 4

1. pair 2. unit 3. odd 4. even 5. zero

Day 5

1. equal 2. word 3. greater than 4. group 5. less than

Review

1. ten + six = sixteen 2. thirteen – nine = four 3. six x three = eighteen 4. zero + fourteen = fourteen 5. twenty – eight = twelve

Week 26

Day 1

1. shape 2. square 3. circle 4. triangle 5. side

Day 2

1. 

-triangle

-circle

-cone

-square

-rectangle

Day 3

1. yes 2. yes 3. no 4. yes 5. no

Day 4

1. line 2. circle 3. cube 4. cylinder 5. triangle

Day 5

1. Answers will vary.

Review

1. A triangle has three sides. 2. A square has four corners. 3. Three rectangles have twelve sides in all. 4. A cube has six faces 5. Six cylinders have twelve circles in all.

Week 27

Day 1

1. no 2. yes 3. yes 4. no 5. yes

Day 2

1. ounces 2. miles 3. minute 4. meter 5. cups

Day 3

1. teaspoons 2. ounces 3. pint 4. tons 5. week

Day 4

1. foot – 12 inches 2. yard – 3 feet 3. mile – 5280 feet 4. hour – 60 minutes 5. minute – 60 seconds

Day 5

1. one foot 2. three feet 3. one pound 4. sixty minutes 5. seven days

Review

1. teaspoon 2. miles 3. dollars 4. pounds 5. years

Week 28

Day 1

1. part 2. slash 3. numerator 4. bottom

Day 2

1. numerator 2. whole 3. denominator 4. part 5. number

Day 3

1. yes 2. no 3. yes 4. yes 5. yes

Day 4

1. set 2. half 3. third 4. numerator 5. whole

Day 5

1. one-eighth – 1/8 2. two-tenths – 2/10 3. one-half – 1/2 4. three-sixths – 3/6 5. one-fourth – 1/4

Review

1. three 2. thirds 3. equal 4. five

Month 7 Review

A

J	X	C	O	U	N	T	C
S	U	M	D	S	U	J	D
G	Z	E	Q	U	A	L	I
A	S	V	Y	B	O	P	V
D	W	E	Q	T	E	R	I
D	E	N	R	R	A	E	D
I	Q	K	J	A	L	S	E
O	A	P	F	C	P	B	G
P	V	X	D	T	A	N	H
M	U	L	T	I	P	L	Y

B 1. three 2. inches 3. twelve 4. sixty 5. four

C 1. line 2. circle 3. diamond 4. cone 5. corners

Week 29

Day 1

1. upstairs 2. bicycle 4. remember 4. repair 5. whistle

Day 2

1. globe 2. sphere 3. above 4. highways 5. directions

Day 3

1. map 2. city 3. direction 4. compass 5. blue

Day 4

1. west 2. seas 3. capital 4. north 5. roads

Day 5

1.

S	N	O	R	T	H	L	W
O	K	E	A	S	T	S	E
U	H	A	G	T	W	A	S
T	A	S	T	A	T	E	T
H	C	B	N	C	A	R	K

Review

1. way 2. route 3. road 4. red 5. high

Week 30

Day 1

1. polideman 2. leader 3. vote 4. law 5. mayor

Day 2

1. elect 2. White House 3. president 4. rule 5. vote

Day 3

1. brave 2. careful 3. goodness 4. proud 5. truth

Day 4

1. president 2. works, White House 3. obey, laws 4. United States, country 5. Congress, laws, country

Day 5

1. cheat 2. honor 3. fair 4. honest 5. neat

Review

1. B 2. E 3. A 4. C 5. D

Week 31

Day 1

1. marry 2. birthday 3. respect 4. obey 5. family

Day 2

Answers will vary.

Day 3

1. harvest 2. feast 3. Hanukkah 4. lights 5. Posadas

Day 4

1. turkey, stuffing, (Thanksgiving) 2. (Ramadan), chicken, fig cake 3. (Las Posadas), fruits, candy 4. potato pancakes, (Hanukkah) 5. (Kwanzaa), nuts, fruit

Day 5

D	A	D	B	R	O	T	H	E	R
A	S	I	S	T	E	R	P	Y	M
K	B	K	O	L	P	Q	R	A	O
G	R	A	N	D	M	A	T	U	M
F	K	L	M	P	Q	Z	F	N	D
T	U	N	C	L	E	B	R	T	U

Review

1. father 2. grandfather 3. sister 4. brother 5. aunts

Week 32

Day 1

1. cheese 2. fruit 3. egg 4. cherry 5. sandwich

Day 2

1. pizza 2. pancakes 3. lemon 4. carrot 5. hot chocolate

Day 3

1. waffle 2. potato 3. beans 4. pancake 5. watermelon 6. any sentence using the correct word

Day 4

1. cookie 2. picnic 3. crackers 4. fruit 5. diner

Day 5

1. dinner 2. knife 3. plate 4. peas 5. cake

Review

1. dishes 2. chicken 3. pumpkin 4. sprinkles 5. berry

Month 8 Review

A

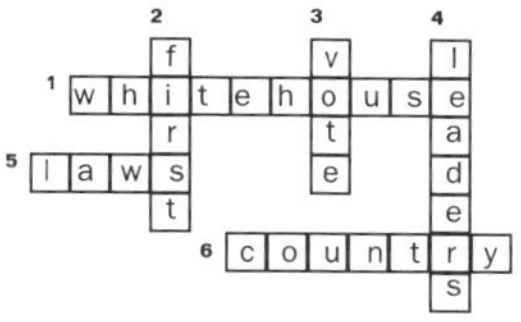

B. 1. president 2. citizens 3. branches 4. country 5. stars

Week 33

Day 1

1. yes 2. yes. 3. no 4. yes 5. no

Day 2

1. truck 2. tracks 3. traffic 4. airports 5. bicycle

Day 3

1. sailboat – wind 2. car – gasoline 3. subway – electricity 4. rowboat – muscles 5. airplane – jet fuel

Day 4

1. automobile – garage 2. train – station 3. helicopter – heliport 4. sailboat – dock 5. jet – airport

Day 5

1. school bus 2. subway 3. taxi, airport 4. train, station 5. sailboat, wind

Review

1. taxi 2. station 3. train 4. subway 5. airport

Week 34

Day 1

1. yes 2. yes 3. no 4. yes 5. no

Day 2

1. C 2. D 3. B. 4. E. 5. A

Day 3

1. crossing guard 2. school bus 3. principal's office 4. cafeteria 5. students, playground

Day 4

1. chalk 2. read 3. workbook 4. gym 5. ruler

Day 5

1. chalkboard 2. lunchroom 3. playground 4. classroom 5. backpack

Review

Answers will vary; any sentence using the correct word

Week 35

Day 1

1. click 2. fizz 3. bow wow 4. buzz 5. swish

Day 2

1. boot 2. sink 3. roof 4. miss 5. loan

Day 3

1. squeak 2. crunched 3. hiss 4. Smack! 5. Crackle, crackle, pop!

Day 4

1. oink 2. growl 3. neigh 4. moo 5. pounding

Day 5

1. barked 2. howled 3. giggled 4. hoot 5. squished

Review

1. quack 2. baa 3. hoot 4. purr 5. ring

Week 36

Day 1

1. team 2. winner 3. finish 4. ball 5. score

Day 2

1. baseball 2. soccer 3. forward 4. basketball 5. score

Day 3

1. right field 2. home plate 3. captain 4. catcher 5. goalie

Day 4

1. place 2. helmet 3. football 4. glove

Day 5

1. catcher 2. pitcher 3. boater 4. climber 5. jumper 6. any sentence using the correct word

Review

1. gloves 2. field 3. team 4. batter 5. skates

Month 9 Review

A

B	A	S	E	B	A	L	L
G	O	C	H	R	U	N	O
O	S	O	C	C	E	R	S
A	B	R	W	I	N	T	E
L	A	E	T	R	A	C	K
F	O	O	T	B	A	L	L

B 1. win 2. coach 3. team 4. foul 5. score

C 1. game 2. ball 3. run 4. team 5. track